By Ac(

Disclaimer

The information provided in this book is designed to provide helpful information on the subjects discussed. The author's books are only meant to provide the reader with the basics knowledge of a certain topic, without any warranties regarding whether the student will, or will not, be able to incorporate and apply all the information provided. Although the writer will make his best effort share his insights, learning is a difficult task and each person needs a different timeframe to fully incorporate a new topic. Neither this book, nor any of the other author's books constitute a promise that the reader will learn a certain topic within a certain timeframe.

Learn Javascript In A DAY

The Ultimate Crash Course to Learning the Basics of the Javascript Programming Language In No Time

Table of Contents

Preface: Who, What and Why JavaScript?

If you're reading this book, chances are that you're just starting out with front end development. Front end development has come a long way since the early days of the web and now isn't just limited to basic HTML. Its impossible to imagine front end coding without JavaScript nowadays, JavaScript is everywhere and is pretty much a staple for all web applications.

Gone are the days where simple HTML was all you needed to get started with building a compelling website. Static HTML has been phased out and the demand of the hour is feature rich web content, which is impossible without incorporating effective JavaScript.

Who is this for?

This book makes a few assumptions that you have a basic understanding of HTML and how static HTML webpages are coded. We also assume that you know a bit of css and you are relatively quite new to JavaScript. Even if you have some primary knowledge of coding in JavaScript, this book will serve as a welcome refresher to re-enforce key concepts as well as introduce concepts you may not be well acquainted with, which would definitely improve your coding skills.

This book won't make you a JavaScript ninja overnight, not even if you read through the book ten times over and complete all the exercises in it, and we don't even aim to do so. The boundaries of programming which define the gurus and ninjas from newbies are redefined on a daily basis. This book will definitely avail you of the core concepts required to use JavaScript after which learning advanced concepts would become second nature. You will learn the best practices for coding in JavaScript as well as core programming concepts that are mandatory to becoming a better coder.

Once through the book you would have an indepth understanding of how to program in JavaScript as well as have completed a series of exercises that would walk you from basic introductory concepts to a full fledged real world situation. At the end of the book, you'll work on a practical application making use of all the skills you've learnt during the course of the book.

What is JavaScript?

Let's start from the top, what exactly is JavaScript to begin with. JavaScript is a client-side scripting language. In the domain of web development you have client side languages and server side languages. Server side languages are languages that are used to code pages that are parsed and executed on the server and include languages such as

Php, ASP, ASP.NET and Ruby to name a few.

Client sided languages are executed or run in the browser - hence the name client. The 'client' in this case the browser makes a request to the server which in turn 'serves' the HTML which is displayed to you. Every time you enter a web url in the url box of your browser, you're sending a request to a server which in turns send back a mesh of HTML which is displayed to you in your browser. Your browser parses the HTML and displays it to you.

What can JavaScript do?

As stated JavaScript is coded to run in the client side, so it runs in your browser. It is because of JavaScript that web pages do not have to be static any more. JavaScript enables web pages to show a lot more interaction than merely clicking on a link to open a new page. And this is something you've obviously noticed in almost every website you've visited. Like for example:

- Those annoying pop ups that ask you for your phone number and email
- The time on pages which seems to tick in sync with your clock
- Those form fields lighting up in red when you enter something wrong
- Those awesome fade in and slide through animations
- Those websites which apparently seems to

remember your preferences from a recent visit

•Those lists that seem to update on their own without refreshing the page when you click the submit button

All that and more is on account of JavaScript. One more key aspect of client side scripting with JavaScript is also to reduce the number or volume of requests that would be made to a server. For example consider the following situation:

You need to take in visitors name, email and message into a guestbook form on a website. To make sure that users enter the correct details you've coded into your server side script - lets assume its php - a basic validation module that checks to make sure every guestbook entry submitted is correctly filled out i.e. emails are a valid email and the name is a real name. If someone enters a wrong entry your server has to run the validation and then send back the same page with an error message asking him to enter it again. If along with the server sided code, you also code using JavaScript on the page itself a similar validation script that checks the entries BEFORE the form is submitted - you not only reduce the number of HTTP requests made to the server but you also save the end user from having to wait until after a form is filled and submitted to find out he's made a mistake.

This was a very simple example - think how mad you would make an end user if the form was exceptionally large and he was on a slow connection.

Why should I learn JavaScript?

To put it bluntly, JavaScript is perhaps the first programming language any developer must learn. To put it even more bluntly its integral for anyone who's even partially serious about being in web development to know JavaScript before even considering any other scripting language be it client side scripting or back end server sided scripting. Here is a few reasons why:

Easy to Learn & work with

Seriously, JavaScript is dead simple to learn and is a pleasure to work with. You don't need a lot to get started with JavaScript and as you code you can instantaneously see the results of your work. This is totally unlike coding using server sided scripts such as Php & ASP where you definitely need a server to execute your script on. With JavaScript all you need is a browser and you're ready to go.

JavaScript can do anything that HTML can't

JavaScript give you the power and flexibility to allow the end user to manipulate the content on your webpage. With JavaScript you can validate content entered in a form, allow the end user to change content on the page and even interact with elements on the page itself. You can also set code to be executed on different events such as what happens if someone clicks a button or hovers over a picture or moves away from the page or even tries to close the page. In short you have a lot of control over how and what the user can interact with giving a whole new dimension to your web pages.

User Experience Depends on it

Getting back to our example with the huge form, imagine a user on a really slow connection, who's really depressed. He finds this counsellor's website where he has to enter a message as well as a valid phone number. The poor guy types out all his life woes, on how his girlfriend left him for his best friend, how he defaulted on his car payments, the foreclosure notice he's received as well as the leaky faucet that's given him sleepless nights - but in all that he forgets to enter a valid phone number and submits the form hoping for a reply. And for some reason some one forgot to add server sided validation so there is now no way to get back to him. Your user sits back waits a few days wondering why no one has called and ultimately drinks himself half dead assured that no one gives a toss for him in the world.

Ok that was pretty melodramatic but you can see where this is coming from. Websites shouldn't be cumbersome and there isn't much interaction possible with static HTML.

High Demand

JavaScript is high in demand and almost every web developer is expected to know a certain degree of JavaScript. Web development is a lucrative career and its all the more important to be well acquainted with all the tools and technologies that you would ultimately be required to work with. You only have to take a look at Job requirements on Job Boards to see the openings available for people who know JavaScript or are acquainted with one of the many JavaScript libraries that are out there - like jQuery and BackboneJS (More about these bad boys later on in the book)

You'll need it anyway

If you're going to be coding websites and web applications, you will ultimately need to code front end and that is wehre you just cannot do without JavaScript. As mentioned earlier knowing JavaScript is mandatory for being an effective web developer. You can run away from it, avoid it as much as you can but ultimately you will definitely have to stop running and accept the fact that you cannot do without JavaScript.

How long have people been using JavaScript?

JavaScript has been around for quite a while now. It was

originally developed by Brendan Eich at Netscape in the early 90s for the Netscape Communicator Browser. He developed the language aiming to make web pages more dynamic and interactive. Interesting to note that JavaScript doesn't have any co-relation with the Java programming language except that they share the word java.

During this time Microsoft had rolled out their own client sided language called JScript for the Internet Explorer browser. JScript was based on Netscapes JavaScript and was named JScript to avoid copyright issues.

This led to what was known as the browser wars where the leading browsers provided their own implementations of the client side language. This had serious repercussions that you now had proprietary code that was heavily browser based so at times scripts coded to run in a Netscape browser would fail in a Internet Explorer.

To cut a long story short JavaScript has been through major evolutions and has more of less standardized over the history that spans almost two decades. Earlier on users pretty much viewed client sided scripts as an annoyance and browsers at the time even had the option to 'turn client scripts' off. But things have dramatically changed and web applications are wholly dependant on client side scripts for successful execution. With the introduction of AJAX and the resurgence of the Web 2 revolution JavaScript has made a tremendous comeback and is here to stay.

Is it magic? Dangerous?

Depends on what you can use it for, granted that JavaScript allows you a great deal of control over not only the HTML page but also to the users browser, it won't cause a PC melt down so its pretty safe to use.

However there have been a number of security vulnerabilities with Javascript ever since its inception such as Cross site Scripting which enables hackers to return malicious scripts to users which are executed in the users browser. Pretty much like those banner ads that you were warned so many times not to click on, the worst that such scripts can do is access information stored on your browser and that includes authentication details stored in cookies as well as other kinds of data you wouldn't want people to get their grubby hands on.

The onus of protection is on the user in this regards and the most we all can do as decent people is never use the power of JavaScript for evil dastardly deeds - like any super power, in the wrong hands it can spell catastrophe!

<Dramatic music plays in the background>

What do I need to get started?

This is the beauty of working with JavaScript, you can get started right away. All you need is your favourite text editor and a browser. Text editors such as SublimeText, textmate and Notepad plus plus are highly recommended. You can also use an IDE like dreamweaver although that would be a bit of overkill. And if you're really adventurous you can always use good old notepad.

For browsers we highly recommend using Firefox or Chrome as both browsers offer facilities to debug and inspect your code. For this book the exercises have been run on a firefox browser but any browser can be used to test your code.

While it is highly beneficial to install a web server such as apache or IIS on your system - it is not necessary as we won't be doing any bit of server sided coding and instead focusing mainly on front end scripting with JavaScript.

Quick Run Down

So far we've gone over quite a bit about JavaScript such as:

- JavaScript is a client sided language so it runs in the browser
- JavaScript is mandatory for front end development
- It can be used to make static web pages more interactive and dynamic
- There is a huge demand for JavaScript in web based careers.
- Client sided scripting can reduce the load on servers
- JavaScript is just awesome and easy to learn

In the next chapter we'll begin coding in JavaScript and introduce you to the fundamental building blocks of the language as well as get you started on the traditional Hello World application in JavaScript.

Chapter 1: Hello JavaScript

To get started with JavaScript we'll build a traditional Hello world application using JavaScript. During the course of this book, we'll be focusing on learning JavaScript through realtime coding and walking you through the code explaining what it does and how does it work. To get started lets set up your workspace.

Setting up your workspace

As we said, there isn't much required with getting started with JavaScript. To start with fire up your preferred text editor of choice and open your browser.

At this point you might want to consider installing a web server if you wish to do some server sided programming. However for the sake of learning just JavaScript this won't be required. The scope of this book doesn't include the process for installing a web server as there are ample resources to set up a webserver available online.

You might wish to install an apache or an IIS server. For users running windows you can get apache based installables such as WAMP and XAMP which install and configure apache plus php and mysql for you. Alternatively if you have IIS installed on your windows machine that is good enough.

The webserver on your system acts just like any regular

server online only to a smaller scale.

On your webserver you would have a folder to store your website(s). On Apache this folder is normally the:

```
path/to/apache/www
```

Or path/to/apache/htdocs

On IIS the path to this folder would be

```
C:/InetPub/wwwroot
```

..Assuming you have IIS set up in your C drive.

This is referred to as the root folder of your webserver and during the course of this book, any references to the root folder would be to this specific folder irrespective of whether you're running IIS or Apache.

Some Code

In the root folder, create a new directory, lets call it lessons. We'll be storing all our lessons in individual folders within this directory. In that folder create a new directory and give it a name - let's call it lesson-1. Once you've done that fire up your favorite browser of choice and navigate to that directory. Make sure that your server is running and type in the navigation bar of your browser assuming you've:

```
http://localhost/lessons/lesson-1
```

And voila - nothing shows up. This is obvious because we

haven't made a default index page yet. Create a new file in your lesson-1 folder and call it `index.html`.

Add in some basic HTML code:

```html
<html>
  <head>
    <title>Learning JavaScript</title>
  </head>
  <body>
  </body>
</html>
```

This is a barebones HTML page with just the opening and closing body tags. Now let's start off with a basic script.

The <script> tag

Since we're familiar with HTML, its time to take a look at the `<script>` tag. Let's write a basic piece of JavaScript here:

```html
<html>
  <head>
    <title>Learning JavaScript</title>
  </head>
  <body>
    <script language="JavaScript">
      document.write('Hello world');
    </script>
  </body>
</html>
```

Refresh your page in the browser and you should see `Hello World`.

What just happened?

Lets take a look at our code to begin with. All JavaScript code is enclosed within the `<script>` tags. At the moment there is just one piece of code which says:

```
document.write('Hello World');
```

The `document.write` is a function that simply outputs whatever is passed to it. For now a just understand that a function is a piece of code that accepts a parameter and does something. We'll go into indepth detail on functions later on. But for now we should be clear that passing anything to `document.write` would be outputted to the browser.

Also note at the end of the line there is a semi-colon `;`. When writing code in JavaScript all lines of code must end with a semi-colon before the next line of code. This is a syntax requirement and if you've worked with C or C plus plus you might find this very familiar already.

So what happened was that when the page loaded, the script was interpreted by the browser. Lets try this with a few variations.

Document.writing stuff

As noted anything passed to the `document.write` function will be outputted to the browser. Let's output a few lines of text and see what happens. Enter the following code:

```
<script language="JavaScript">
  document.write('Hello there.');
  document.write('I am coding.');
  document.write('Hear me debug.');
</script>
```

Refresh your browser - not exactly what we expected. You see all three strings in the same line even though you made three different calls to `document.write` on three different lines. The fact is that the browser outputs only HTML and in order to give form to any outputted text from JavaScript it also has to be formatted using HTML. Lets rewrite this a bit by enclosing the strings passed with <p> tags:

```
<script language="JavaScript">
  document.write('<p>Hello there.</p>');
  document.write('<p>I am coding.</p>');
  document.write('<p>Hear me debug.</p>');
</script>
```

Refresh the browser and now you see all the strings are on different lines.

Might not seem like much that can't be accomplished with static HTML. So let's try a more interesting example.

```
<script language="JavaScript">
  document.write('You are accessing this page from ' +
location.hostname);
</script>
```

Run this script and you should see it say `You are accessing this page from localhost.`

The `location.hostname` is also a built in function that returns the hostname of the current URL. We used the plus sign above to append it to the text.

Already you can see that there is more to JavaScript that just outputting HTML.

Inline JavaScript vs External JavaScript

The above is an example of JavaScript that has been coded inline. This is where you have your JavaScript enclosed in `<script>` tags in the same HTML page. While this is neat for trying out simple code - its not a very good practice and is not very scalable especially as your page and code grows more complex.

For this reason its best to run JavaScript externally by putting all your JavaScript in its own file or set of files and including it using the same `<script>` tag. To start with create a file in the same folder where you have your `index.html` and call it `main.js`.

Save the file and open it in your text editor and copy paste the code between the script tags (without the script tags) into the `main.js` file and save it.

Remove the script tags and code from your HTML document and within the `<head>` tag add the following rendition of the `<script>` tag:

```
<script language="JavaScript" src="main.js" ></script>
```

Save and refresh your browser - you should see the exact same output as you did when the code was inline. We've moved all the JavaScript to an exclusive JavaScript file (Javescript files are appended with .js) and included that file by making a reference to it in the `<script>` tag above. The `src` attribute of the `<script>` tag points to the location of the file to load.

An even better practice is to put all JavaScript code into its own `js` folder. As your projects grow more complex you'll find that it would make sense to group your JavaScript into different files.

NOTE: YOU CAN ALSO INCLUDE JAVASCRIPT FILES WITHIN THE BODY TAG ALTHOUGH BY CONVENTION THEY'RE OFTEN LOADED IN THE `<head>` TAG.

Summary

We've covered some basic ground here and got a very simple JavaScript application up and running.

We understood how to use the `<script>` tag as well as the difference between inline and external JavaScript files.

In the following chapter we'll touch upon the basic syntax of JavaScript as well as the constituent building blocks which make up the language. You'll be introduced to JavaScript variables and operators as well as practical lessons on how to use them. Plus you'll also get a refresher arithmetic course in the process :)

Chapter 2: The Basics

Now that you're all set up and have had your first taste of an actual JavaScript application, we move on to understanding the basic syntax of JavaScript.

JavaScript is unique in respect that it is an interpreted language as opposed to a compiled language. In programming you have interpreted languages and compiled languages. In an interpreted language the program is executed statement by statement whereas in a compiled language - the entire program is first compiled into a format that can be executed and then is run. A main characteristic of interpreted languages is that if there is an erroneous statement in the program, the statements prior to the erroneous statement would still be run and executed however the program would halt on encountered the erroneous code.

You'll understand why this is important to know later on in the book.

Objective

In this chapter you will learn about JavaScript variables and the different types of variables used in JavaScript code. You will also understand the different operators used such for performing arithmetic and logical functions. At the end of the chapter you will be well versed with the construction of basic expressions using variables and operators.

Core JavaScript Syntax

Think about syntax as grammar and vocabulary for computers. You can't talk much if you didn't have much of a vocabulary and you would definitely make no sense if you had no sense of grammar. The same also applies to computer programming. Like all computer programming languages JavaScript has its own syntax, a set of rules which you must abide by when writing valid code.

JavaScripts syntax is comprised of:

- Variables
- Operators
- Operands
- Comments
- Expressions
- Keywords
- Rules

In our previous code we were introduced to one basic rule of JavaScript and that was:

EVERY STATEMENT MUST END WITH A SEMI-COLON

Note that when we say statement, it doesn't necessarily mean a statement is all code on one line. Whenever you write a statement in JavaScript it has to end with a semi-colon. Even if you write multiple statements on the same line, each statement ends with a semi-colon. For example:

```
var t = 1;var x = 1;
```

This is just as good as writing

```
var t = 1;
var x = 1;
```

Another useful feature in JavaScript code is the ability to add comments to code. Comments are added to give brief explanations of what code actually does. They are only for the programmers reference and are not run as JavaScript code. Comments are added in JavaScript by prepending the comment with two backslashes. This would mark everything on that single line as a comment eg:

```
// This is a comment - it doesn't do anything
var t;    //Everything beyond this is a comment
```

Alternatively comments can be encloses between the characters /* and */ respectively. This way of commenting only excludes the content within the characters as comments. Eg:

```
// This entire line has been commented
/* This bit of text is all commented */
var t = 1; /* This is commented out */ var x = 2;
```

Commenting code is a very good practice and helps to make sense of what complex code does especially if you have to come back to it or if someone else has to work on your code. Keep comments short but comprehensive enough for someone to understand what the code block below is supposed to do.

Variables in JavaScript

The variable is a building block for any program. Variables are used to store data during the program. In JavaScript a variable is defined using the `var` keyword. So to declare a variable in JavaScript you would write:

```
var i;
```

In the above code `i` has been declared as a variable. Its not really doing much now, you can assign values to a variable for use in your code using the = sign. The equals = sign is referred to as the assignment operator:

```
var i = 10;
```

The above code declares a variable called `i` and assigns the number 10 as a value to it. The above bit of code can also be rewritten as this:

```
var i;
i = 10;
```

Now this value can be used in any bit of JavaScript code. Let's go back to our first example to see this in action. Type out in your JavaScript file:

```
var i = 10;

document.write(i);
```

The page now should display the contents of i which is the number 10.

Also you can declare multiple variables on the same line in JavaScript eg:

```
var i, j;
```

Plus you can also assign them values on one line as well so the following is also perfectly valid JavaScript:

```
var i = 10, j = 12;
```

Naming Variables

When declaring a variable you do have a few constraints with regards to how you can declare a variable. Variable name can be made of letters, underscores and numbers but they cannot start with a number and cannot contain a space or special characters. For example the following variable declarations are valid:

```
var i;
var Image;
var module_01;
var M1;
var iM1;
```

However the following variable declarations are invalid and would cause a program error:

```
var 1a;
var module 01;
var module-01;
var i@m1;
```

JavaScript variable names can be as long as you want and can be as small as a single character eg:

```
var this_is_a_very_long_and_humongous_variable_name =
1;
var t = 1;
```

Although when coding it would make more sense to make sure your variable names it inself make sense and aren't too long.

Types of Variables

JavaScript has support for many types of variables. So far we've seen examples where we've only assigned numbers to JavaScript. JavaScript provides support to the following variables:

Numbers

A variable can be assigned a numerical value. JavaScript has support for integers and floats. For example the following is an example of assigning a number to a variable:

```
var num1 = 100; // This is a valid integer number
var num2 = 100.00 // This is a decimal number
```

Strings

Strings are blocks of text. They can be as long as needed and can even be as small as a single character. You can also have an empty value as a string. Strings are always enquoted in single or double quotes whenever it is to be assigned. So the following is valid:

```
var s1 = "This is some text!"; //Assigned a string
var s2 = 'This is also some text';    // Single quotes
work well too
var n = ''; // This is a valid empty string
```

While the following is invalid and would not:

```
var t = This is text; // This will not run - JavaScript
can't tell where the string starts and ends
```

When assigning text that has quotes within, make use of the backslash operator to ensure that the quotes in the string do not cause any issues in assignment eg:

```
var t = 'This work'/s well.';
```

The backslash escapes characters that would otherwise be interpreted differently by JavaScript.

Booleans

A boolean variable contains either a true or false value. Booleans are the most basic types of variables in use. Booleans are useful when working with conditional statements, which we'll touch upon later in the book.

A boolean variable can be assigned as below:

```
var x = true;      //Outputting x will give true
var y = false;     //Outputting y will give false
```

Arrays

Arrays are how multiple values can be stored in a single
variable. Think of them as a list of variables all accessible
by an index. Arrays are declared in JavaScript using the
square brackets with individual values separated by
commas within. Eg:

```
var a = ['oranges', 123, false, 'lemons'];
```

In the above a[0] would
return oranges and a[1] would return 123

We'll touch upon arrays in a later chapter of the book, for
now you just need to know that arrays can also be assigned
to variables.

Objects

Objects are a grouping of different values and functions.
Think of objects as arrays, the only difference is that arrays
are indexed by numbers while objects can have custom
indexes.

Please note that this is a very basic and somewhat crude
definition of objects but should be enough to understand
the example of assigning an object to a variable for now.
Objects will be covered later on in the book.

```
var o = {name:'Bob Jones', age:87, active:true};
```

Operators operator!

Operators are what get things done between variables. JavaScript provides a number of operators. We'll be covering the most commonly used operators which you would need to know for day to day development activities. The operators in JavaScript are categorized as below:

Assignment Operators

We've already used the most common assignment operator used i.e. the = sign. This simply assigns a value to a variable. However there are a number of different assignment operators each with their own specifics.

= The = operator simply assigns a value to a variable without making any change in the value itself.

```
i = 10;
document.write(i);    // Outputs 10
```

+= The += operator functions differently when used with a string and a number. When used with a string it merely concatenates the value onto the string. When used with a number it adds the value to the number:

```
var i = 'Hello ';
i+='Bob';          // i now equals to 'Hello Bob'
```

```
var t = 10;
t+=5;               // t is now 15 - this is just likes
writing t = t + 5
```

-= The -= operator subtracts the value from the variable and stores the resulting value in the variable. This is a shorthand method of writing a subtraction equation. This is used only with numerical values:

```
var t = 10;
t-=2;               // t is now 8 - this is just likes
writing t = t - 2
```

*= The *= operator is shorthand for a multiplication expression and merely multiplies the value with the variable and stores the resulting value in the variable itself:

```
var t = 10;
t*=5;               // t is now 50 - this is just likes
writing t = t * 5
```

/= This divides the variable with a value and stores the result in the variable:

```
var t = 10;
t/=2;               // t is now 5 - this is just likes
writing t = t / 2
```

Arithmetic Operators - JavaScript knows arithmetic!

Arithmetic operators are used to conduct mathematical operations between variables and values. The common arithmetic operators used in JavaScript are:

Operator	Function
+	Addition
-	Subtraction
*	Multiplication
/	Division
%	Modulus
++	Increment
--	Decrement

ADDITION (+)

Addition adds a value to a variable.

```
var a = 10;
var b = 20;

var c = a + b;      // z = 30
```

SUBTRACTION (-)

As the name suggests the value is subtracted from the variable. Note that subtracting a larger value from a smaller one would obviously result in a negative value.

```
var a = 10;
var b = 20;
var c = b - a; //c equals to 10

var a = 10;
var b = 20;
var c = a - b; //c equals to -10
```

MULTIPLICATION - *

The multiplication operator multiplies the value into the variable.

```
var a = 10;
var b = 2;

var c = a * b;      // z = 20
```

DIVISION(/)

This divides the variable by the value. Results can also yield decimal values.

```
var a = 10;
var b = 2;

var c = a / b;      // z = 5

var a = 5;
var b = 10;

var c = a / b;      // z = 0.5
```

MODULUS % the modulus returns the remainder of the variable when divided by the value. So 10%3 would return the number 1. When you use the modulus with an even number and two you would always get zero.

INCREMENTING ++ & DECREMENTING --

The increment operator simply increments the variable by one. Likewise the decrement operator does the opposite and decrements the variable by one.

```
var a = 10;
a++; // a is now 11
a--; // a is now 10
```

This is a short hand for the assignment operator +=1 and −=1 respectively.

Comparison Operators

Probably the most commonly used operators you would be using are the comparison operators. Whenever you would need to make a decision based on the value of a specific variable you would make use of comparison operators.

JavaScript currently provides the following comparison operators:

Operator	Description
==	equal to
===	equal value & type
!=	not equal
!==	not equal value or not equal type
>	greater than
<	less than
>=	greater than or equal to
<=	less than or equal to

How do they work?
You might recognize most of the comparison operators

above from basic arithmetic comparisons. Lets go over them one by one.

(==) EQUALS TO

The equals to operator does as its namesake. It compares two variables and returns a Boolean value `true` if both variables have an equal value and return s `false` if not. Keep in mind that `==` is not the same as`=` where `=` is an assignment operator.

```
var a = 10; // a is now assigned the value 10
var b = 15; // b is now assigned the value 15

a == b;    // returns false
b == a;    // also returns false whichever way you put
it

a == 10;    // returns true
a = 15;     // a is now assigned the value 15
a == b;     // returns true
```

(===) EQUALS IN VALUE AND TYPE

This might seem like someone put one too many equals to sign, but the `===` operator checks both variables and returns true if both the variables are of the same value and type. For example in JavaScript the values `10` and the values `'10'` might be of a similar value but are definitely not the same type as the latter is a string type because it is enclosed in quotes and the former is an integer.

```
var a = 10; // a is now assigned the numerical value 10
var b = '10'; // b is now assigned the a string value
'10'

a == b;    // returns true
```

```
a === b;     // returns false

var a = '10'; // a is now assigned the a string value
'10'
b === c; // returns true
```

(!=) NOT EQUAL TO, (!==) NOT EQUAL TO IN TYPE AND VALUE

When it comes to the comparison operators when the first = sign is replaced with a the Exclamation mark ! symbol, it denotes the opposite of what the original operator was intended for. So == when it becomes ! = now compares for variables that are not equal to each other while ! == checks for variables that are not equal to each other in terms of value as well as type, because sometimes equality is not what you're looking for.

```
var a = 10; // a is now assigned the numerical value 10
var b = '10'; // b is now assigned the a string value
'10'

a != 10;     // returns false
a != 15;     // returns true

a === b;     // returns false
a !== b;     // returns true
```

(>/<) THE GREATER THAN AND LESS THAN OPERATORS

In basic mathematics you're probably aware of the > greater than and the < less than symbols, which check if variables on either side of the symbol are of greater or lesser values. They work pretty much the same way in JavaScript. Note that in JavaScript comparing a string witha numeric value such as `'10'` with a number using the above operators is perfectly allowed.

```
var a = 10, b = '10';

a > 5;      // returns true
a < 5;      // returns false
a > '5';    // returns true

a < b;      // returns false
```

(>=/<=) - GREATER THAN OR EQUAL TO / LESS THAN OR EQUAL TO Following on from primary arithmetic, the >= greater than and equal to operator as well as the <= less than or equal to operator does exactly as their name sake.

```
var a = 10, b = '10';

a >= 5;      // returns true
a >= 10;     // returns true
a <= 10;     // returns true
a <= 11;     // returns true
a >= b;      // returns true
a <= b;      // returns true
```

Logical Operators

Logical operators always return a Boolean `true` or `false` value. They are used to check between two or more statements for logical connectivity. These operators are used in tandem with other operators as displayed earlier on. The logical operators used in JavaScript are:

Operator	Description
&&	logical 'AND'
' '	logical 'OR'
!	logical 'NOT'

(&&) - AND THERE WAS ...

The logical AND operator checks between two variables or statements to make sure both collectively return a Boolean true. The statement when evaluated with an AND operator much evaluate to a Boolean true value. For example:

```
var a = 10, b = '10';

(a == 10) && ( b=='10');    // returns true
(a > 10) && ( b=='10');     // returns false
(a >= 10) && (true);    // returns true

(a >= 10) && (b=='10') && (true);    // returns true
```

This is useful if you wish to check if more than one statement are evaluated as true. This would be highly used especially when we would be working with conditional statements.

(||) - AND THERE WAS ...

Sometimes you need to evaluate if just one out of a set of statements evaluated as true. The Logical Or operator denoted by two pipe symbols does exactly that. Were a logical AND operator will return true if all the statements evaluated returned true, the OR operator returns true only if one out of a single statement would evaluate as true.

```
var a = 10, b = 12;

(a == 10) || ( b==10);      // returns true
(a > 10) || ( b==10);       // returns false
(a >= 10) && (true);        // returns true
```

*(!) - The logical NOT symbol

As explained earlier the ! symbol works in tandem with other symbols and expressions and returns the opposite of what those statements would evaluate to. For example

```
var a = 10;

(a == 10);      // returns true because a is equal to 10
!(a == 10);     // returns false negating the statement
a equals 10
(a == 11);      // returns false because a is not equal
to 11
!(a == 11);     // returns true negating that a is not
equal to 11..got that?
!(!(a == 11));  // returns true negating the negating
that a is not equal to 11..please don't do this?
```

Conditional Operators

JavaScript provides one conditional operator which makes an assignment based upon a simple decision. This is the ? : operator. To understand check the following example:

```
var a = 10;
var b = (a == 10 ? 12 : 0); // b is assigned 12
```

The above statement reads if a is equal to 10 then return

the value 12 else the value 0. Since a is equal to 10 then the variable b is assigned the value of 12. This is a very handy shortcut for making assignments based upon a single statement. You can make the statements as complex as you wish for example:

```
var a = 10, b = 12;
var c = (a == 10) && (b > 10) ? 12 : 0; // c is
assigned 12
```

As in the above statement we have a logical AND operator checking between two expressions within the conditional statement. A word of advice is whenever you use the conditional operator keep it simple other wise you might end up in a situation like this which can be pretty difficult to handle:

```
var c = !((a == 10) && (b > 10)) || !((b < 15) &&
((c/2) < b)) ? 12 : 0; // please don't do this
```

String Operators - work on strings

When working with strings, you'll need to do more than just check if two strings are the same. While you can use the ==, === operators to check if two strings are equal, working with strings is obviously a lot different than working with numbers. Which is why JavaScript provides a few native string operators which you would definitely find use of in your day to day programming. We'll touch more on string operators when we cover strings in a later chapter.

Built in JavaScript functions - good to know

Before we proceed further it's important that we get acquainted with a few handy built in functions that JavaScript provides us. These functions are native to JavaScript and are very useful or terribly annoying depending on how you use them.

Alert - everyone loves/hates the alert

This is a very simple function that opens a rather rude alert box with a message you can pass to it. The syntax is very simple:

```
alert('Hello there!');
```

This should open up an alert box with the message 'Hello there!' and an OK button to close it. While this is a native JavaScript function, we'll be using it a bit throughout further examples. But in a real time setting you would do best to refrain from using it too much as it is more of an annoyance to users.

Confirm - what do you want to do today?

One of the more useful functions -
the `confirm` command actually opens a confirm box with the choice to click on a Yes or No button. This is useful to quickly get confirmation from the user. Here is a quick example:

```
if(confirm('Can I say yes?')== true){
  document.write('Yes');
}else{
  document.write('No');
}
```

Running this will open a confirm box with the message passed. Clicking on OK will run the code block in the If statement printing out Yes while clicking cancel will do other wise. The confirm function returns true if the user confirms and false if the user doesn't. A very handy function to get quick confirmation from the end user and is a very good example of how easy it is to interact with the user.

Prompt - enter something please

This command is used to actually get some user input from the user. Running this opens up a prompt box where the user is 'prompted' to enter some information. For example:

```
var name = prompt('What is your name?');

if(name != ''){
  document.write('Hello ' + name);
}else{
  document.write('You didn\'t enter your name!');
}
```

The above code prompts the user to enter his name, the entry from the user is taken in the name variable. This is a very simple example of interaction from the user and the application responding to client interaction.

Summary

We've covered a lot of ground here and have gone over:

- Variables, the different types of variables that JavaScript supports
- Assignment operators
- Arithmetic operators
- Logical Operators
- Conditional Operators

Chapter 3: Conditions conditions and more conditions

In the last chapter we touched upon the different variable types as well as the core syntax for constructing an expression in JavaScript. We should be able to make use of the basic operators to conduct mathematical and logical evaluations. But coding is more than just fancy arithmetic and logical dribble. Just like in life, everything doesn't move in a straight line, the same applies to coding - you need to to almost make make room for a detour or exception.

Objectives

In this chapter you will learn about the various conditional statements used in JavaScript to execute code based on specific conditions. The conditions would make use of operators learnt in the previous chapter. We'll touch upon the different conditional statements and make use of a real life practical application to understand their usage.

The - IF - condition

The most basic and fundamental conditional statement you can use in JavaScript. There is no piece of code on earth that doesn't involve an IF statement at some point. The If statement is construed as follows:

```
if(expression){ // if expression evaluates to true run
the code in brackets
  //code here
}
```

The if statement checks if an expression is true and then executes the code in the enclosed brackets. This is similar to the conditional operator that we used in the previous chapter only its a bit more readable. Here is an example of an if statement

```
var a = 10;
if(a == 10){
    document.write('Booyah');
}
```

The above code checks if the statement a==10 evaluates to true, which it does and then prints out the word Booyah. The If statement can check more than one expression at the same time.

```
var a = 10, b = 12;
if((a == 10)&&(b==12)){          // evaluates true so the
code is executed
    document.write('Booyah');
}

if((a > 1)&&(b<12)){  // evaluates as false
    document.write('Booyah Again'); // this is never
printed
}
```

As we learnt earlier on the usage of logical operators, we can now see their practical applications in the conditional

statement. Just like the logical operators here is an
example of the NOT operator used in an IF statement

```
var a = 10, b = 12;
if(!(a == 10)){          // returns false
    document.write('Booyah');   // this is never run
}


if(!(a < 10)){           // returns true
    document.write('Booyah');   // this runs
}
```

The code block within the IF statement is regular
JavaScript code. Here is an example of the IF statement
mimicking the conditional operator.

```
var a = 10, b = 12;
var c = 0;

c = a == 10 ? 11 : 0;
if(a == 10){  // this is the same as writing the above
    c = 11;
}
```

The conditional IF statement makes for better reading than
the conditional operator although with the conditional
operator you can execute a conditional statement on one
line. You can also do the same with the conditional IF
operator provided you understand that all individual
statements and expressions in JavaScript end with a
semicolon. So the following is perfectly valid JavaScript:

```
var a = 10;
var c = 0;

if(a == 10){c = 11;} // this works - but doesn't read
too well
```

There's also an - else - to that

The If statement can be written on its own, however in case you wish to evaluate code should the IF statement not be successfully evaluated then that is where JavaScript allows you add an `else` statement to that.

```
var a = 10;
var c = 0;

c = a == 10 ? 11 : 0;
if(a == 10){   // now this is completely the same as
writing the above
    c = 11;
}else{
    c = 0;
}
```

The else statement extends on the conditional statement enabling the following block of code to be executed only if the If statement fails. So the following bit of code is not the same as the code above.

```
var a = 10;
var c = 0;

c = a == 10 ? 11 : 0;
if(a == 10){
    c = 11;
}

c = 0; // this will always run as it is not in an
enclosed if - else statement
```

The above code is not a complete if - else statement. The expression at the bottom c = 0; is not bound to any logical statement i.e. it will run whether or not a equals 10 or not. Any code that needs to be executed when the expression in the IF statement doesn't evaluate put it in the corresponding else statement.

Here is a more practical example:

```
var name = '';
if(name == ''){
  document.write('Name cannot be blank!');
}else{
  document.write('Your name is ' + name);
}
```

The statement checks if the name variable is empty, in which case it outputs an error message. The same logic can be rewritten in the following way:

```
var name = '';
if(name != ''){
  document.write('Your name is ' + name);
}else{
  document.write('Name cannot be blank!');
}
```

Here the If statement checks if the name variable isn't empty -its all up to how you wish to implement the logic in your system. At the same time it's also possible for you to write this statement with out the IF-Else statement and using just the conditional operator we spoke of earlier.

```
var name = '';
document.write((name != '')?'Your name is ' + name :
'Name cannot be blank!');
```

You can see how malleable and versatile the JavaScript language is, we can achieve the same logic using a conditional operator - although it makes for difficult reading and is not a good practice. Try and ensure that you don't have too much going on per line of code. It will save you many endless hours of debugging woes as your code gets more complex.

You can also attach another if condition to your - else statement further on extending the conditional statement. The Else - clause is run if the expression in the IF statement doesn't evaluate to true. However you can add a further if and else statement if you wish to be more specific. For example:

```
var name = '';
if(name == ''){
    document.write('Name cannot be blank!');
}else if(name == 'Bob'){          // the name isn't
empty check if it is Bob
    document.write('Your name is Mr. Bob');
}else{        // the name is neither empty nor is it
Bob
  document.write('Your name is not Bob but ' + name);
}
```

The above statement runs a second if statement when the first one fails. You can daisy chain if statements this way one after the other to check for for specific conditions as per your requirements.

NOTE THE SPACE BETWEEN THE ELSE AND THE FOLLOWING IF STATEMENT, NOT LEAVING A SPACE WOULD BE AN ERROR AND YOUR CODE WOULD NOT RUN.

Nesting Conditions

Imagine a situation, now we're going to consider more practical situations here on. You need to check if you have ten eggs and further more if they're fresh or not. You could work out something like this:

```
var number_of_eggs = 10;
var eggs_are = 'fresh';

if((number_of_eggs == 10)&&(eggs_are == 'fresh')){
   // do something
}
if((number_of_eggs == 10)&&(eggs_are != 'fresh')){
   // do something
}

if((number_of_eggs != 10)&&(eggs_are == 'fresh')){
   // do something
}
if((number_of_eggs != 10)&&(eggs_are != 'fresh')){
   // do something
}
```

That can work but it seems a bit insane to have to make four different conditional statements to check for every single possibility. An easier way to do this is to nest your if - else statements within each other. Just like any code you can also nest an if - else statement. Take for example the above code can be rewritten as:

```
var number_of_eggs = 10;
var eggs_are = 'fresh';

if(number_of_eggs == 10){
   if(eggs_are == 'fresh'){
     // do something
```

```
  }else{
    // do something
  }
}else{
  if(eggs_are == 'fresh'){
    // do something
  }else{
    // do something
  }
}
```

Not bad, we have one statement checking one condition and further conditions are checked within the statements. Although in the above example you may notice that the nested if statement is getting duplicated. This will be overcome when we get to using functions in a later chapter. However for now you just need to understand how nested conditional statements work.

At this point you may be tempted to wonder, why do we even need to make use of an else statement when you can accomplish the above without the else statements. The above could well be written as below:

```
var number_of_eggs = 10;
var eggs_are = 'fresh';

if(number_of_eggs == 10){
  if(eggs_are == 'fresh'){
    // do something
  }
  if(eggs_are != 'fresh'){
    // do something
  }
}

if(number_of_eggs != 10){
  if(eggs_are == 'fresh'){
```

```
    // do something
  }
  if(eggs_are != 'fresh'){
    // do something
  }
}
```

Seemingly the above would work perfectly fine, however there is a problem with the above approach. When an If statement evaluates to true, only the code within that IF statement would be executed and the corresponding code in the following else block would not. This way you only check for whether the expression in the IF statement is valid once and then you don't need to check it again to make sure it's false. In the above example you would be running a minimum of 4 comparision expressions as opposed to only two in the one preceding it with an else statement. This makes a huge difference in terms of performance as your applications grow.

KNOW THIS - ELSE IS YOUR FRIEND!

The conditional switch statement

As and as your conditional statements get more and more complex, you'll want to use more than just an if else statement. The if and else statement work fine when you need to check a variable for a few possible values or a few expressions. But what do you do when you need to check a variable for a lot of possible values? We're not talking about checking if a variable is true or false or empty or not.

What if you were to check a variable for any number from 1 to 10. Assume you have a set of error codes and you wish to display a differnt message for each code. With an If statement you'd probably have to write something of the following:

```
var code = 101;

if(code == 100){
    // do something
}else if(code == 101){
    // do something

}else if(code == 102){
    // do something

}else if(code == 103){
    // do something

}else if(code == 104){
    // do something

}else if(code == 105){
    // do something

}else if(code == 105){
    // do something

}else if(code == 106){
    // do something

}else{
    // do something
}
```

This is a fairly effective way of checking for more than one possible value but JavaScript allows for a much easier syntax to accomplish the same requirement, albeit in a less painful way.

Say hello to the `switch` statement.

The switch statement does exactly what the above if statement does only with less of a code overhead i.e. not as much code and brackets to write out. The syntax of a typical switch statement would be as follows:

```
switch(variable){
  case value:
  break
  default:
  break;
}
```

The above code could be rewritten in a switch statement as below:

```
var code = 101;

switch(code){
    case 100:
        // do something
    break;

    case 101:
        // do something
    break;

    case 102:
        // do something
    break;

    case 103:
        // do something
    break;

    case 104:
        // do something
```

```
        break;

    case 105:
        // do something
        break;

    case 106:
        // do something
        break;

    default:
        // do something
        break;
}
```

It's definitely much cleaner and more readable. For ever possible value you would wish to check for you would check it with a `case` statement. The last `default` statement is akin to the final else statement in the previous example, where you would run code in case none the variable didn't check against any of the values in all the case statements. The `break` statement in JavaScript especially when used in the `switch` statement breaks out of the code block being executed so you're saved from having to run the code through multiple blocks of code.

What makes the switch statement more efficient than the previous If statement is that in a switch statement the expression is evaluated only once, where as in an if statement its evaluated wherever there is one.

Here is a different variation of the switch statement, lets assume that you want to execute the same block of code if the value of `code` variable is 101, 102 and 105. The switch statement can be re-evaluated as:

```
var code = 101;

switch(code){
    case 100:
        // do something
    break;

    case 101:
    case 102:
    case 105:
        // do something
    break;

    case 103:
        // do something
    break;

    case 104:
        // do something
    break;

    case 106:
        // do something
    break;

    default:
        // do something
    break;
}
```

In the above example, we've excluded the break statement from the case statements where the values are both 101,102 and 105. This ensures that the same code block is run whenever the variable matches one of the above numbers. You don't need to repeat the same block of code now in different case statements in case you need to run the same code in multiple situations.

When you have to make complex decisions

Conditional statements help when you need to run code based on conditions. In programming, you would definitely come across situations where certain conditions are more complex than other conditions. Such conditions may warrant extensive use of the above conditional statemnts or even a combination of the switch and if else statement. For example imagine a situation where you need to check for different error codes and then decide whether you need to send an email to the user or output a warning based on whether the user is an administrator or a visitor. You can always use if-else statements within switch case blocks. Lets look at the following example.

```
var code = 101;
var user_role = 'admin';

switch(code){
    case 100:
        // do something
        if(user_role == 'admin'){
          // do something
        }else{
          // do something
        }
    break;

    case 101:
    case 102:
    case 105:
        // do something
        switch(user_role){
            case 'admin':
            // do something
            break;
```

```
        case 'visitor':
        // do something else
        break;
    }
    break;


    default:
        // do something
    break;
}
```

The above code shows how you can nest both if statements
and even further switch statements within a switch
statement. Although this is a bit of an extreme example
and there are better ways of testingsuch complex
expressions, nevertheless this should give you an idea of
how using switch and if-else statements, you can within
JavaScript build complex applications that react based on
different conditions.

Lets order a Pizza

Whose up for some Pizza, jokes aside - let's make a simple
script that goes through the process of ordering a Pizza.
We're all familiar with our favorite fast food takeaway, so
the process is pretty straight forward.

First lets decide what kind of crust do we want. We'll ask
the user for the kind of crust he wants.

```
var crust = prompt('What kind of crust do you want -
thin or regular?');
```

The user gets to enter the kind of crust he wants - but wait
what if he enters something we don't have? We need to
check the crust entered.

```
var crust = prompt('What kind of crust do you want -
thin or regular?');

if((crust == 'thin') || (crust=='regular')){
    var cheese = prompt('Choose your cheese?');
    switch(cheese){
        case 'mozarella':
        case 'feta':
        case 'parmesan':
        case 'cheddar':

        break;
        default:
            alert('Sorry we do not have that kind of
cheese.');
        break;
    }

}else{
    alert('Sorry we do not serve that kind of crust
here.');
}
```

Pretty sweet, now lets assume that if he wants cheddar
cheese, he can have a tomatoe sauce based Pizza, else if
chooses any other cheese he would have a white parmesan
sauce based Pizza.

```
var crust = prompt('What kind of crust do you want -
thin or regular?');

var sauce; // we initialized a sauce variable

if((crust == 'thin') || (crust=='regular')){
    var cheese = prompt('Choose your cheese?');
```

```
switch(cheese){
    case 'mozarella':
    case 'feta':
    case 'parmesan':
        sauce = 'tomato';
    break;
    case 'cheddar':
        sauce = 'white';
    break;
    default:
        alert('Sorry we do not have that kind of
cheese.');
    break;
    }

}else{
    alert('Sorry we do not serve that kind of crust
here.');
}
```

Now that is done - lets output the details of the Pizza he ordered.

```
var crust = prompt('What kind of crust do you want -
thin or regular?');

var sauce; // we initialized a sauce variable

if((crust == 'thin') || (crust=='regular')){
    var cheese = prompt('Choose your cheese?');
    switch(cheese){
        case 'mozarella':
        case 'feta':
        case 'parmesan':
            sauce = 'tomato';
        break;
        case 'cheddar':
            sauce = 'white';
        break;
        default:
            alert('Sorry we do not have that kind of
```

```
cheese.');
        break;
    }

    alert('You ordered a Pizza with '+crust+' crust, '+
cheese + ' cheese and '+sauce+' sauce');

}else{
    alert('Sorry we do not serve that kind of crust
here.');
}
```

Run the code and it seems fine, but wait something is
wrong. If you enter the wrong kind of cheese you still get
an alert that tells you what kind of Pizza you ordered
without the sauce. We need to put a check here to make
sure that only to output the details of the ordered pizza if
the sauce is entered with a valid entry. For this let's change
the code a bit and assign the sauce variable a value when
the wrong sauce has been entered and run a check before
we output the correct entries.

```
var crust = prompt('What kind of crust do you want -
thin or regular?');

var sauce = -1; // we initialized a sauce variable with
a default value to check against

if((crust == 'thin') || (crust=='regular')){
    var cheese = prompt('Choose your cheese?');
    switch(cheese){
        case 'mozarella':
        case 'feta':
        case 'parmesan':
            sauce = 'tomato';
        break;
        case 'cheddar':
            sauce = 'white';
```

```
        break;
        default:

            alert('Sorry we do not have that kind of
cheese.');
        break;
    }
    if(sauce!=-1){    //as long as the sauce variable
isn't the original -1 we can assume that all correct
values were entered.
        alert('You ordered a Pizza with '+crust+'
crust, '+ cheese + ' cheese and '+sauce+' sauce');
    }
}else{
    alert('Sorry we do not serve that kind of crust
here.');
}
```

Now that is better, you can now see how in a real practical example with a few simple conditional statements how we were able to control the flow of a script based upon input from the user. As we proceed, we'll work with more complex problems and work out best practices on dealing with them.

Summary

- We learnt the concept of conditional statements as well as how JavaScript evaluates different statements.
- We understood that an expression has to evaluate to true in order for a conditional statement to be evaluated.

- We learnt about the if and else statement as well as how conditional statements can be nested.
- An alternative to complex if statements are the switch and case statement which allows checking a single variable for multiple possible values.

Assignment

Exercise 1

Write a script that checks if an integer variable is bigger or less than 100. It should output the result stating the difference. So if the number 60 is checked, the output should say '60 is less than 100 by 40'. Take the variable from the user using the `prompt` command.

Exercise 2

Expand on the Pizza example above. Have the user also input their choice of sauce using a prompt command. The User first chooses his choice of crust, then his choice of cheese, and then he should enter his choice of sauce. Check against the sauces 'white pesto', 'Signature tomato', 'cheesy garlic', 'caeser dressing' and 'pasta sauce'. Use a switch statement.

Chapter 4: Do it once then repeat - loops

During development, many a time you would come across situations where you'll need to repeat the same block of code or at least have to make refernces to the same bit of code over an over again. For example you might want to initialise 10 variables with the same number or in a sequence however having to type out 10 different declarations and assignments is repetitive and it defeats the purpose of having to use a programming language in the first place.

All programming languages come with the inate facility to repeat blocks of code that you would otherwise have to manually write out the number of times you would want to have them repeated. JavaScript is no different and it also comes with its own set of 'loop' statements as they are called to make repeated recurrances of code blocks as you would require.

Overview

In this chapter we would introduce you to the concept of looping in JavaScript. You would be acquainted with the different loop statements such as the for loop, while loop as well as the do, while loop. You would understand the differences in these loop statements as well as the practical implications of their differences and touch upon some examples.

A world without loop statements

Think a world without photocopy machines, or cupcake holders - no two cupcakes would ever look the same. It would be catastrophic in a way. When it comes to programming, imagine a situation where you need to output some text a 100 times. Lets assume you've been punished for driving in a no driving zone(whatever that is) and you have to write out 1000 times 'I will not drive in a no driving zone'. You've been allowed the use of JavaScript during the course of your punishment (don't ask just assume) and you can't copy paste anything. You could do it the insanely wrong and mindless way of having to write out a document.write statement 1000 times as so...

```
document.write('I will not drive in a no driving
zone.<br/>');
document.write('I will not drive in a no driving
zone.<br/>');
document.write('I will not drive in a no driving
zone.<br/>');
document.write('I will not drive in a no driving
zone.<br/>');
document.write('I will not drive in a no driving
zone.<br/>');
document.write('I will not drive in a no driving
zone.<br/>');
document.write('I will not drive in a no driving
zone.<br/>');
```

```
// this will take forever
```

Or better yet you could have the programming language do it for you. Meet the loop statement! Loops are an integral part of all programming languages such that they allow you to execute a block of code repeatedly for a set number of times or until a specific condition is met.

Loops are extremely useful, especially in cases more practical than the example quoted above. We'll go over the basic loop statments in JavaScript and apply some real life examples as well as some not so real life examples(such as the one above) and see how loops work.

The for loop

The most basic and versatile loop statement in JavaScript is the for loop. The syntax of the for loop is as below:

```
for (statement 1; statement 2; statement 3) {
    //Code to be run
}
```

Statement 1 is an expression that is executed before the loop actually starts. This is normally an initialization expression that would initialize a variable to be used as a counter.

Statement 2 is an expression that defines the condition under which the code would run i.e. the code would keep on running as long as the expression in statement 2 evaluates to true.

Statement three is an expression that runs over each iteration of the loop.

These three statements in the for loop define how many iterations are there going to be which means how many times the code in the for loop block would run. So if we were to output the above example lets say 10 times we would write our for loop as so:

```
for( i = 0 ; i < 10;   i++){
   document.write('I will not drive in a no driving
zone.<br/>');
}
```

The result is that the statement 'I will not drive in a no driving zone' is printed out 10 times. Lets deconstruct the for loop a bit. We can see that statement 1 is i = 0, we've initialized the variable i with zero. The variable i would serve as a counter during the loop. Statement 2 outlines a condition which is i < 10 which means keep iterating while the variable i is less than 10. So we know that the variable i has been initialized with a starting value of zero and the loop would run until the variable i is no longer less than 10 i.e. equals to or is greater than 10. The third statement i++ is run whenever the loop iterates and at each iteration of the loop we're incrementing the variable i by one.

You might be wondering why we initialized I with zero and not the number 1. We could do that but then we would have to adjust statement 2 to be i<=10 otherwise the statement would be executed only 9 times. This is because the i++ statement increments the value of i after an iteration.

So if we were to repeat the code block within the for statement 20 times we would just change the statement 2 to `i < 20`. Since the for loop is very versatile, you can use just about any set of statement provided that they effectively work as a loop. For example the following for loop would not run at all:

```
for( i=0 ; i==0; i++){
    //do something
}
```

This is because the second statement's condition has already been fulfilled before the loop has even begun. And the following loop would just never end:

```
for( i=0 ; i<0; i++){
    //never ending loop
}
```

Because in the above loop, the iterative statement of `i++` would never at any point assign `i` a value that would be less than zero as `i++` increases the value of `i` by one in every iteration. So you need to be very careful when working with loops. One of the cardinal sins of working in JavaScript is putting an alert command within an finite or infinite loop, doing the latter would nevertheless earn you the scorn of web users the world over so please never use any of the commands that warrant bringing up a pop up in a loop.

Lets loop at a few variations on the for loop.

At this point it's interesting to note that all the three

statements in a JavaScript for loop are completely optional.

You can easily omit the first statement provided you have already initialized the variable used in the for loop before the for loop itself. So the following code is perfectly valid:

```
var i = 0;
for( ; i < 10;  i++){
   document.write('I will not drive in a no driving
zone.<br/>');
}
```

Just remember that even if you omit a statement in the for loop, make sure you still have the corresponding semi-colon. That tells JavaScript which statement has been omitted.

Likewise the second statement i.e. the condition under which the loop runs can also be omitted. However if you omit the second statement you must provide a way to break out of the loop within the loop itself. This can be done by using the break statement as used in the switch case statement in the previous chapter together with a conditional if statement. So the above code can be rewritten as below:

```
for( i = 0 ; ;  i++){
   if(i < 10){
      break;
   }
   document.write('I will not drive in a no driving
zone.<br/>');
}
```

If you fail to add a break within the code somewhere after

omitting the second statement you'll end up with a loop that will never end. This is one situation you'll definitely want to avoid.

Similarly the third statement i.e. which is run in every iteration can also be omitted - provided you make a provision within your code to iterate the variable used as a counter in the for loop. So the same code can be rewritten as:

```
for( i = 0 ; i < 10 ;){
    i = i + 1;
    document.write('I will not drive in a no driving
zone.<br/>');
}
```

Continue - not just break!

While we know that the break statement does as its namesake i.e. breaks completely out of the loop or block of code its in, at times you would want to skip an iteration but not necessarily stop the loop or break out of the block of code. Like lets assume you would want to run the above code but when the variable i would equal 5 you would not want to print for some reason. One way is that you use a large if statement:

```
for( i = 0 ; i < 10 ;i++){
    if(i != 5){
        document.write('I will not drive in a no driving
zone.<br/>');
    }
}
```

This is one way of doing it but there is a better way of doing this that won't have you enclose large blocks of code in brackets. Enter the `continue` statement.

The `continue` statement skips the current iteration such that any code following the continue statement is not executed for that iteration when the continue statement is run. So the above can be easily rewritten as:

```
for( i = 0 ; i < 10 ;i++){
    if(i == 5){
        continue;
    }
    document.write('I will not drive in a no driving
zone.<br/>');
}
```

While - you were looping

The while loop is another loop native to JavaScript. Unlike the for loop the while loop takes only one statement i.e. a condition under which the loop runs. A typical while statements syntax is as below:

```
while(expression){

}
```

There are no initialization statements and neither are there any incremental statements in the while loop. All of that has to be handled within the code block it self. If we were to write a while loop with the condition to keep iterating while `i` is less than 10 as below:

```
while(i < 10 ){
  document.write('I will not drive in a no driving
zone.<br/>');
}
```

You'll notice that we get an error - it seems that the variable i hasn't been initialized. in JavaScript you need to initialize a variable prior to using it. So lets make the following amendment.

```
var i = 0;
while(i < 10 ){
  document.write('I will not drive in a no driving
zone.<br/>');
}
```

Running the code we see that its running and running and it just won't stop! Why's that you may wonder? The fact is that we've defined a condition but made no provision that the condition can even be met. The value of i stays the same i.e. zero through out the code. So where do we put our iterator? Within the block of code to be iterated.

```
var i = 0;
while(i < 10 ){
  document.write('I will not drive in a no driving
zone.<br/>');
  i++;

}
```

The above code works exactly as the early for loop. Its a matter of preference what loop you may use from the two. It's obvious to see that with the for loop, initialization, running condition and the iteration code is encouraged to be part of the for loop itself while in the while loop it can be spread out and not necessarily be intrinsic to the while loops declaration.

do -- while - one more loop for you

The do while loop is a variation of the while loop such that in a while loop and even in the for loop, the condition is tested before the loop is run while in a do while loop the condition for execution of the loop is tested after the iteration. This means that a do while loop will run at least once even if the loop is evaluated as false.

The basic syntax of the do while loop is as below:

```
do{
// code to be executed
}while(expression)
```

Just like the while loop, you need to initialize the variable used in the condition before the loop itself and put the code to iterate the variable within the code block. Otherwise you would end up with code that either won't run in case the variable isn't initialized, or code that just won't stop until its crashed your browser, that is if you haven't defined an iterator. The above example could be rewritten in a do while loop as below:

```
var i = 0;
do{
  document.write('I will not drive in a no driving
zone.<br/>');
  i++;

}while(i < 10 )
```

The only difference between the do while statement and the while statement can be seen in the following example.

```
var i = 0;
while(i != 0 ){
  document.write('While loop runs.<br/>');
  i++;
}

var i = 0;
do{
  document.write('Do while runs.<br/>');
  i++;

}while(i !=0 )
```

We've set the condition for both loops to stop incrementing when the variable i equals zero - in this case the variables have already been initialized with zero so the condition has already been met before the loop even runs. However that is true for the while loop, in the case of the do while loop - it's plainly seen that the code block is executed before the condition is even tested. So the result is that the while loop will not run at all, but the do while loop would run at least once before testing the condition.

Nesting Loops

Just like nesting conditional statements, we can also nest loops in JavaScript. A nested loop is when you have a loop within another loop. To demonstrate this we'll use JavaScript to make a table with a set number of rows and cells using two loop statements. Let's make it more interesting we'll print out a multiplication table while we're at it. Let's look at the following code:

```
var tbl = '';
tbl = '<table>';
tbl = tbl + '</table>';
document.write(tbl);
```

This doesn't do much but let's look at the above code, we've introduced a simpler way of outputting large amounts of text. Rather than use a document.write statement for everything we need to write to the screen, we assign our string data to a variable. Note that with strings the + operator works as a concatenator and thus concatenates strings to form a new string. In the above code we've just created a simple<table> element with no rows and cells. Let's use a loop to add 10 rows to our table.

```
var tbl = '';
tbl = '<table>';
for( i = 1; i <= 10; i++ ){
   tbl = tbl + '<tr>';
   tbl = tbl + '</tr>';
}
tbl = tbl + '</table>';
document.write(tbl);
```

Not bad now lets create some cells. Remember we need to create ten cells for every row. This can be accomplished by nesting another loop within the loop that creates the rows.

```
var tbl = '';
tbl = '<table>';
for( i = 1; i <= 10; i++ ){
   tbl = tbl + '<tr>';
```

```
for( j = 1; j <= 10; j++ ){
    tbl = tbl + '<td>';
    tbl = tbl + ( i * j );
    tbl = tbl + '</td>';
}

    tbl = tbl + '</tr>';
}
tbl = tbl + '</table>';
document.write(tbl);
```

Note that in the nested loop we used a different variable j for the iteration so that we don't mix up the iteration variables between the two loops. Let's analyze the code and see how it works.

We have the first for loop, we'll call this the outer loop because it contains another loop. When the outer loop runs it runs the inner loop within it ten times, for every time the outer loop runs it creates a row on each iteration so we get ten rows. At the same time whenever the outer loop runs, on each iteration it runs the inner loop. The inner loop runs ten times in each iteration of the outer loop i.e. the inner loop has its own iteration going on and that is how we end up with ten cells for every row. The multiplication is simply done by multiplying the outer loops iterative variable with the inner loops iterative variable.

The same loop could have been recreated with a while loop.

```
var tbl = '';
tbl = '<table>';
var i = 1;
while(i <= 10){
    tbl = tbl + '<tr>';
```

```
var j = 1;
for( j <= 10){
  tbl = tbl + '<td>';
  tbl = tbl + ( i * j );
  tbl = tbl + '</td>';
  j++ ;
}

tbl = tbl + '</tr>';
i++ ;
}
tbl = tbl + '</table>';
document.write(tbl);
```

The above code accomplishes exactly what the for loop
based code before it does. The only difference is that with
a while loop you need to increment the iterative variable
your self as well as initialize it before referring to it in
code.

Summary

- We learnt that code blocks called loops are used to
run code repetitively.
- All loops have a condition to be evaluated against
which terminates the loop when met.
- If a loop's condition doesn't evaluate to true, it will
result in an infinite loop and can crash your page.
- The "For" loop, while loop and do while loop are
the basic loop statements available to JavaScript.
- The do while loop is unique in that the condition

for the loop is evaluated after the loop is run meaning it will run at least once.

Assignment

Exercise 1

Write a script that takes a number from the user using the prompt command. Loop through the number and output to the screen at every iteration whether the current number is even or odd.

Exercise 2

Using nested loops, create a calendar view for a single month of thirty days. For this make a table with seven columns the headers of which correspond to the days of the week. List out in each cell a number which would correspond to the day so you get a table that resembles:

sun	mon	tue	Wed	thu	fri	sat
1	2	3	4	5	6	7
8	9	10	11	12	13	14
15	16	17	18	19	20	21

sun	mon	tue	Wed	thu	fri	sat
22	23	24	25	26	27	28
29	30					

Chapter 5: Functions - Don't put it all in one place!

While we've checked on loops in the previous chapter for repeating blocks of code, you would always require similar code in more than one place. Coding the same code block whenever you need it is very redundant and also defeats the purpose of programming in the first place. This is why programming languages provide functions as a solution to reusing blocks of repeatable code. A function is a block of code that is coded once and can be executed by making a call to the function. JavaScript provides support for functions and we'll go over the various ways how functions are defined in JavaScript and how they give programming structure.

Overview

In this chapter we'll understand how to declare a function and the variations of calling a function. We'll also discuss how to pass parameters to functions and how functions can be used to return values. We'll also touch on the concept of scopes with regards to variables and their practical implementation.

Why functions?

In a few words, no one likes to repeat themselves. Its a fact that when you would be programming you will almost always find yourself requiring the make use of the same or similar blocks of code in all of your applications. Like if you wish to check if an email is valid, calculate a percentage, convert between different numerical formats - you'll find yourself repeating a lot of code. Now this opens up a pleatora of possibilities for errors to take place and will make your code obviously very long and highly repetitive.

Functions are blocks of code that you code just once and then whenever you need them you can always make a call to the required function. Infact you've already used a few functions so far without even knowing it.

A basic function

Functions are declared by using the `function` keyword followed by the name of the function - circle brackets and the code in enclosed curly brackets. A function can be named in pretty much the same way as a variable is named i.e. they consist of only alphanumerics and underscores and cannot start with a number. The example below is an example of a function that returns a message.

```
function greet(name){
```

```
    return 'Hello ' + name;
}
```

Functions can accept parameters and can return values. In the above example the function called `greet` accepts a parameter called `name`. The `return` keyword does two things, first it breaks out of the function and secondly returns a value whenever the function is invoked. The above function can be invoked as below:

```
greet('Bob');
```

Running this code doesn't appear to do anything, because the function has returned a value and we havent done anything with it. Let's capture the value returned by the function in a variable.

```
var greeting = greet('Bob');
document.write(greeting);
```

In the above example the `greeting` variable is assigned the value retunred by the `greet()` function in this case, we passed the string 'bob' to the function. The function returned 'Hello Bob' and since we've printed that to the screen using document.write - you would see it on the page. This is roughly how functions work. Prior to this we've actually made use of a few native JavaScript functions which act the same way as the function defined above.

A few native JavaScript functions

In our previous chapters we were introduced to some core native JavaScript functions such as the alert, confirm and prompt functions. All these functions take in parameters and return values similar to our simple example. For example when making a call to confirm:

```
var a = confirm('Are you sure?');
```

We pass in a parameter namely the message to be displayed in the confirm popup box, and the function in return shows the box, captures the users selection and returns either a true or false value based on the users selection. This is also the same with the prompt function.

Assigning a function to a variable

In JavaScript there is more than one way to declare a function. A function can also be assigned to a variable - technically it would still be a function declaration. For example the above function could very well be rewritten as below:

```
var greet = function(name){ return 'Hello '+name; };
```

Keep in mind that when invoking a function that it is always invoked with () following it. If you try to invoke a function without the following brackets - it returns the entire definition of the function. So in the above example:

```
var greet = function(name){ return 'Hello '+name;};

document.write(greet('Bob')); // prints 'Hello Bob';
document.write(greet); // prints function(name){ return
'Hello '+name;};
```

Once a function has been declared it can be further
assigned to another variable. For example:

```
var greet = function(name){ return 'Hello '+name;};
var g = greet;

g('Bob'); // is the same as greet('Bob');
```

This is a subtle yet huge difference that the () brackets
can make when working with functions. Functions allow
you to reuse the same code with different variables. If you
have a bit of code that would obviously be used again or
completes a set of functionality on its own - it's a good
idea to put it into a function and make a function call.

Passing parameters to functions

Functions would not be of much use if you couldn't get
customized results from them. Parameters passed to
functions are accessible within the function by the
parameter name given to the parameter during the
declaration. In JavaScript you have the choice to declare
the parameters to be passed or not to declare. In the above
example we explicitly mentioned the name of the first
parameter to be used during the scope of the function i.e.
in this case name. So you could pass any variable to the

function, but within the function it would be referred to by the name the function was declared with.

You can pass as many parameters as declared to the function. For example:

```
function add(num1, num2){

    return num1 + num2;
}

add(2,3); // returns 5
```

Any parameter you've declared in the function declaration can be referred to by the name it was declared with like in the above example the two parameters passed to the function are num1 and num2 respectively. If for some reason not all of the function parameters are passed:

```
function add(num1, num2){

    return num1 + num2;
}

add(10) //
```

The above would yield an error because num2 has not been passed a value and is hence undefined. Alternatively you can also pass more than the declared number of parameters such as:

```
function add(num1, num2){
    return num1 + num2;
}

add(10, 12, 34, 5, 33) //
```

In the above example we've passed more than the declared

parameters but they cannot be referenced in the function because we haven't declared for them any name in the function definition. However this won't cause an error. To access such parameters we would make use of a built in JavaScript Object which is accessible to all functions called the `arguments` object. We'll talk in detail about Objects in a later chapter but for now just understand that an Object is a special piece of code that has variables and defined functions. The arguments Object is actually an array which corresponds to all the parameters that have been passed to a function. Lets rewrite our `add` function to take in an unlimited number of parameters using the newly discovered arguments object.

```
function add() {
    var total = 0;
    for (var i = 0; i < arguments.length; i++) {
        total+= arguments[i];
    }
    return total;
}

add(2, 55, 88, 90, 17, 100, 23);
```

In the above example we looped through the arguments array - know that an array is a sequential list of values each accessible through a numeric index. The arguments.length tells us how many parameters have been passed so we can loop through the entire arguments array. Each element in the array of arguments is accessed by the index it is at so argument [0] returns the first element in the array and so forth. We'll talk in detail about arrays in the next chapter but for now you can see how versatile functions in

JavaScript can be.

The recursive function

Recursion is an important concept in programming, this is where a function invokes itself. A number of mathematical expressions would warrant a situation where simply making a function call with a loop is just not possible. Forexample if you were to create a function that would calculate the factorial of a number, the factorial of a number is calculated by multiplying all the numbers from 1 to the number in question. You could calculate the factorial with a loop as below:

```
function factorial(num){
    var result = num;
    while (num-- > 2) {
        result *= num;
    }
    return result;
}

factorial(10);
```

The above function perfectly calculates the factorial of a number greater than 2. If we were to do away with the while loop and code a recursive function we would have the following code:

```
function factorial(num){

    if (num == 0) {     // The factorial of zero is
always one
        return 1;
```

```
    }else {
        return (num * factorial(num - 1));
    }
}

factorial(10);
```

A recursive function needs a conditional statement that would break the cycle of recursion - in this case once the num value passed to factorial becomes 0, the factorial function is no longer called and thus the function returns the final result. Recursion can be a bit daunting at first, and it's easy to accidentally code a recursive function that doesn't know when to stop calling itself resulting in an infinite loop. Recursion is normally favoured over loop statements as it tends to simplify code.

Scoping?

While working with functions we know for a fact that we can access variables that have been passed to the function. And we can also access variables within the function which have been explicitly declared. So in the following example:

```
function foo(name){
    var i = 0;
    // do something

}
```

The variable name and the variable i is accessible by code within the function. This is defined as Local scope - we say that the variables defined within a function have local scope as they are accessible only by code within the function. So in the below example:

```
function foo(name){
    var i = 12;
    // do something

    document.write(i); // prints the value of i

}

document.write(i); // prints nothing
```

The local variable is only accessible within the function and not by code outside the function. Local variables exist when a function is invoked and are destroyed when the function is done with.

However let's consider the following example:

```
var stuff = 12;

function foo(name){
    var i = 0;
    // do something

    document.write(stuff); // prints the value of stuff

}
```

How could the function access the variable stuff which was declared outside the function? Variables declared out side functions on the page have what is called the Global scope. Such variables can be accessed in any function. The variable can not only be accessed but also modified by functions as well without having to even explictly pass it.

```
var stuff = 12;

function foo(){
    // do something
    stuff = 15;
}

foo();
document.write(stuff); // prints 15
```

At the same time you can also declare a global variable
from within a function. To do so you just have to assign a
value toa variable without explicitly declaring it using
the var command. For example:

```
function foo(){
    // do something
    stuff = 15;
}

foo();
document.write(stuff); // prints 15
```

In the above example declaring the stuff variable
without the var command automatically makes it a global
variable which is accessible anywhere in the script. One
drawback of this is that you can pretty much end up
modifying a variable without even knowing it. So try to
make sure that any variables you use are initialized and
that your variables have descriptive names.

Summary

●Functions are blocks of reusable code that can be invoked at will instead of having to write the same code again and again.

●Functions can accept parameters

●By default all parameters of a function can be accepted using the arguments array which is automatically passed to every function.

●Functions can also return values based on the code executed.

●A recursive function is one which calls itself, with recursive functions the function invokes itself until a certain condition is evaluated.

Assignment

Exercise 1

How much do you earn in a day if you work 8 hours? Create a function that takes an hourly rate and outputs the amount you would make in a month if you work 8 hours everyday.

Exercise 2

In the previous chapter you ran a conditional statement to check if a number entered was larger than or greater than 100. Recreate the functionality with a function.

Chapter 6: Arrays - nicely lined up!

At times you need to work on more than just a single variable. The idea of a single variable holding a single value cannot hold true in many rel life examples. A carton of eggs may be regarded as a single unit but then again - so is each and every egg in the carton. A block of houses might seem like a single unit, but each and every single house on that block is also a unit accessible in its own right. Very soon you'll understand that there has to be a better way to collate values than assigning them to an individual variable.

Overview

In this chapter we will touch upon the concept of Arrays and how arrays are implemented in JavaScript. We will look at array declarations, the benefits of using arrays as well as the various traversal techniques used to go through arrays. During this chapter you will be acquainted to the Array object. Through usage of the Array Object you will also be introduced to the concept of using Objects in JavaScript.

The concept of arrays

So far we've used variables that would hold a single value. This might have worked well for all the examples and situations we've come across but practically there would be many instances where you would need to access multiple values through a single declared variable. Much like the concept of houses - you can consider each house on a street accessible by the individual address of the house on that street. However you cannot ignore the fact that the street itself provides an access to each individual house on it. So your house might have a specific address but when you talk about it in reference to the street its on you would say its the 'nth' house on the street.

This is pretty much how arrays work in programming language. An array is simply a variable which contains more than one value. Arrays help i programming when you need to collect multiple values that are associated to each other in some way and store them for access in a single variable.

Creating Arrays

Arrays are declared many like variables are and the same restrictions apply to declaring arrays as you would apply to variables.

```
var gender = ['male', 'female'];
```

In the above example we've declared an array called gender using square brackets and within the array we've stored two values namely 'male' and 'female'. If we didn't have any arrays we'd have to use variables like this:

```
var male_gender = 'male';
var female_gender = 'female';
```

It would have gotten very complicated if we'd require more complex examples. Like if we had to list down different pets:

```
var pet1 = 'dog';
var pet2 = 'cat';
var pet3 = 'rabbit';
var pet4 = 'hamster';
var pet5 = 'bird';
```

Pretty messy and using that in code would have been nightmarish to say the least. If you had to loop through all the types of pets would you create a variable for each pet? Plus what if you had to store not four or five but hundreds of values. What if you're taking values from an external source - you can't put them all in individual variables that is programming suicide! Hurrah for arrays, they allow you to store as many values as you wish under a single variable name.

```
var pets = ['dog', 'cat', 'rabbit', 'hamster', 'bird'];
```

When declaring arrays it doesn't need to be all on one line, line breaks are perfectly allowed in declaring arrays so the following is also perfectly fine:

```
var pets = ['dog',
            'cat',
```

```
        'rabbit',
        'hamster',
        'bird'];           // now that is easy to read
```

That is awesome but how can we access the values in the array? In an array you can access the individual values by referring to an index. The index of the array starts from zero meaning the first element in any array in JavaScript is always at the index of zero. So keep the above example in mind.

```
pets[0]; // equals 'dog'
pets[1]; // equals 'cat'
```

This also means that in an array the last index would equal one less than the total number of elements in the array - so in the above example the last element of the array which has a total of five elements would be.

```
pets[4]; //equals 'bird'
```

The Array object

We can declare an array using the square brackets as above listing all of the individual elements.

Alternatively we can also declare an array making use of the new Array syntax.

```
var pets = new Array();
```

The above code creates an array in the same way as the previous example did. The only differance is that we've used the keyword new to create a a new array Object from the JavaScript Array Class. We'll talk more about classes and Objects in the next chapter. To understand this a bit we must know that a class in programming is code that defines an Object. An Object is an instance of code that has defined a class. Objects have functions and variables called methods and properties respectively.

Any array you create in JavaScript gets with it a set of properties and functions that are helpful in working with the array.

The length of an array

The `length` property of an array returns the number of elements in the array. A very useful property which can help especially if you would want to loop through the array.

```
var pets = ['dog', 'cat', 'rabbit', 'hamster', 'bird'];
pets.length; // equals 5
```

Adding/appending/prepending stuff to an array

Once you create an array you're not stuck with the same array for the length of your code. There are a few ways of adding elements onto an array. Remember that you can always access an array through its index - the same way you can add more elements onto an array using the array's length property itself so in the above example.

```
var pets = ['dog', 'cat', 'rabbit', 'hamster', 'bird'];
//pets.length was 5 and the last index before this was
4 hence we just added a new element onto the end of the
array
pets[pets.length] = 'turtle';
```

But that is not all, you can also modify elements within the
array itself by accessing elements through the index. They
work just like regular variables only this time with an
index.

```
pets[0]; // equals dog
pets[0] = 'Iguana';
pets[0]; // equals Iguana

pets[3]; // equals hamster
pets[3] = 'Goldfish';
pets[3]; // equals Goldfish
```

Alternatively the array object itself provides a few
methods that allow us to add elements onto the array itself.

Pushing/Popping Oh My

When dealing with arrays we know that arrays are
variables where values are stored in a sequential manner.
Adding elements and removing elements from arrays are
referred to as Pushing and popping respectively. The array
object gives us two methods aptly
named push and pop respectively to carry out these
functions.

The push method pushes or adds a new element to the
end of the array. So in the above example where we added

an element to the end of the array we could rewrite it as:

```
var pets = ['dog', 'cat', 'rabbit', 'hamster', 'bird'];
pets.push('turtle'); // returns 5
pets[5]; // equals 'turtle'
```

The same way if we need to remove the last element from the Array we would use the pop method.

```
var pets = ['dog', 'cat', 'rabbit', 'hamster', 'bird'];
pets.pop(); // returns 'bird'
pets; // equals ['dog', 'cat', 'rabbit', 'hamster'];
```

As with functions the push method returns the new length of the array while the pop method returns the element of the array that was 'popped' out.

Shift/Unshift - and these are not gears

Similar to the push and pop methods we also have the shift and unshift methods which pretty much do the same thing in JavaScript so the above two examples can be rewritten using shift and unshift as:

```
var pets = ['dog', 'cat', 'rabbit', 'hamster', 'bird'];
pets.unshift('turtle'); // returns 5
pets[5]; // equals 'turtle'
```

```
var pets = ['dog', 'cat', 'rabbit', 'hamster', 'bird'];
pets.shift(); // removes the last element 'bird' and
returns it
pets; // equals ['dog', 'cat', 'rabbit', 'hamster'];
```

Removing elements from an array

When it comes to removing elements from an array, we're already now aware of the shift and pop functions, however these functions only work by removing elements off the end of the array. You would need to remove elements that obviously aren't always at the further extreme of the arrays you work with.

Removing elements from arrays is pretty similar to modifying and reading them i.e. you would refer them with the index the element is at. To remove an element from an array we use the `delete` command:

```
var pets = ['dog', 'cat', 'rabbit', 'hamster', 'bird'];
delete(pets[1]);
pets; // equals  ['dog', undefined, 'rabbit',
'hamster', 'bird']
```

While delete does delete the value in the array, you're then left with an an undefined value in the same array. Using delete leaves holes in your arrays which isn't exactly the same as how you'd want to remove an element from an array thus shortening it. To do so we have a multifunctional function called `splice`. Splice is a functional method all arrays have that can be used to both delete and well as add elements to an array. Let's take a look at it removing elements:

```
var pets = ['dog', 'cat', 'rabbit', 'hamster', 'bird'];
pets.splice(1,1);

pets; //equals ['dog', 'rabbit', 'hamster', 'bird'];
```

What just happened here? you're probably wondering. In the above example splice takes in two parameters. The first parameter is the position in the array where you want to add or remove an element. The second parameter is the number of elements to be removed. In the above example we removed one element from the arrays index of one thus shortening the array by one element. The splice function can also delete more than one element using the same parameters.

```
var pets = ['dog', 'cat', 'rabbit', 'hamster', 'bird'];
pets.splice(2,2);

pets; //equals ['dog', 'cat', 'bird'];
```

That is all handy dandy but how does splice add elements to array at the same time as well as delete elements? To add elements we can pass in a few more parameters to splice.

```
var pets = ['dog', 'cat', 'rabbit', 'hamster', 'bird'];
pets.splice(2,0, 'turtle', 'goldfish');

pets; //equals ['dog', 'cat', 'rabbit', 'turtle',
'goldfish', 'hamster', 'bird'];
```

The splice method is an example of how JavaScript functions can take in multiple parameters without having to explicitly declare them. In the above example, the first parameter states where to add the element, the second parameter is how many elements to remove and the rest of the parameters are the elements to be added to the array. You can pass in just about any set of parameters as you wish, you can even pass in arrays and objects. An array

can pretty much carry any type of information. At the same
time you can also remove and add elements from the array
using a single splice function:

```
var pets = ['dog', 'cat', 'hamster', 'bird'];
pets.splice(2,1, 'turtle', 'goldfish');

pets; //equals ['dog', 'cat', 'turtle', 'goldfish',
'hamster', 'bird'];
```

It works like glue!

JavaScript provides a very useful function in cases when
you would want to concatenate all the elements of an array
into a string with a delimiter. So if you want a comma
separated string of all the names of pets in the pets array as
above:

```
var pets = ['dog', 'cat', 'hamster', 'bird'];
var names = pets.join(','); // equals
'dog,cat,hamster,bird'

var pets = ['dog', 'cat', 'hamster', 'bird'];
var names = pets.join(' or '); // equals 'dog or cat or
hamster or bird'

var pets = ['dog', 'cat', 'hamster', 'bird'];
var names = pets.join(' and '); // equals 'dog and cat
and hamster and bird'
```

The join function takes one parameter - the delimiter
with which to 'glue' all the elements of the array together.
This is very useful for printing out contents of arrays as a
string - if you try to print out an array

using `document.write` it'll only print out the word 'Array'. Try it out with a few simple arrays.

Combining arrays

How about concatenation more than one array? You have two or more different arrays and would want to join them like a centipede to have a bigger mega-array. Arrays in JavaScript provide the `concat` method which does exactly that. It takes as a parameter any number of arrays and 'daisy chains' them to the original array.

```
var pets = ['dog', 'cat', 'hamster', 'bird'];
var more_pets = ['iguana', 'turtle', 'goldfish'];
var even_more_pets = ['rabbit', 'gerbil'];

pets.concat(more_pets, even_more_pets); // equals var
pets = ['dog', 'cat', 'hamster', 'bird', 'iguana',
'turtle', 'goldfish', 'rabbit', 'gerbil'];
```

Looping through arrays

Since we know that arrays have numerical indexes we can traverse through an array using a loop using the iterator to check for the index. Here are a few examples of iterating through the above array using the different loops that JavaScript has to provide.

```
var pets = ['dog', 'cat', 'hamster', 'bird', 'rabbit',
'turtle', 'goldfish'];
```

```
// the for loop
for(var i = 0; i < pets.length; i++){
  document.write(pets[i] + '<br/>'); // prints out the
element on a new line
}

// the while loop
var i = 0;
while( i < pets.length ){
  document.write(pets[i] + '<br/>'); // prints out the
element on a new line
  i++;
}

// do while works just as well
var i = 0;
do{
  document.write(pets[i] + '<br/>'); // prints out the
element on a new line
  i++;
}while( i < pets.length )
```

In the above examples we did the same thing with all three
different loops. JavaScript however also gives another
special kind of loop for looping through arrays and objects
called the - for..in loop. It works very similar to the
other loops except you don't really need to use a variable to
iterate through the loop and instead it reliese on the Array
or Object its looping through entirely to know when to
stop the loop.

```
var pets = ['dog', 'cat', 'hamster', 'bird', 'rabbit',
'turtle', 'goldfish'];

// the for in loop
for(i in pets){ // i is the index of the array at each
iteration
  document.write(pets[i] + '<br/>'); // prints out the
```

```
element on a new line
}
```

The above loop functions exactly as the other loops, only this time the iterator i takes on the index of the array as it iterates. The actual implication of this function will be appreciated when we work on Objects in the next chapter.

Sorting arrays

Very so often you would want to be able to sort the elements in an array. Its natural like lining up kids at school from the shortest to the tallest during a march parade. With sorting arrays, JavaScript provides the `sort` function which works well on arrays with textual data.

```
var pets = ['dog', 'cat', 'hamster', 'bird', 'rabbit',
'turtle', 'goldfish'];
pets.sort() // equals now ['bird', 'cat', 'dog',
'goldfish','hamster', 'rabbit', 'turtle' ];
```

Along with the `sort` command JavaScript also provides the `reverse` function to totally reverse the order of elements in the array.

```
var pets = ['dog', 'cat', 'hamster', 'bird', 'rabbit',
'turtle', 'goldfish'];
pets.sort() // equals now ['bird', 'cat', 'dog',
'goldfish','hamster', 'rabbit', 'turtle' ];
pets.reverse() // equals now [
'turtle','rabbit','hamster','goldfish','dog', 'cat',
'bird'];
```

This works pretty awesome lets try it with an array that has numerical values:

```
var a = [10, 3, 2];
a.sort() // equals now [10, 2, 3]; huh?
```

How did that happen? Does the `sort` function not know how to count? The `sort` function actually sorts alphabetically treating all the elements of the array as a string instead of a number. So as a string '10' comes before '2' because the number '1' is seen as a preceding '2' - the numerical value of '10' is ignored in this context. To get around this the sort function takes as a parameter a whole function(yes you can also pass functions as parameters - isn't JavaScript grand) for comparison.

This comparison function would take two parameters which would conform to two values that would be compared to each other. Simply stating the `sort` function would call this function every time it would compare two values in the array. With this function you can define how to actually sort the array, as long as the function returns a negative, positive or zero value. Lets look at an example here to do a numeric comparison:

```
var a = [10, 3, 2];
a.sort(function(x, y){return x-y});
```

In the above example we passed a function which subtracts the first element passed from the second. If the first element is greater than the second i.e. the following - the value returned would be positive and thus the element would have its place replaced with the lower element. This sorts the elements numerically from lowest to the highest. The same function can be redone a bit to sort from the highest to the lowest:

```
var a = [10, 1, 2];
a.sort(function(x, y){return y-x});
```

Search search

With arrays having multiple elements, we need to know a way to find a specific element. We can always run a loop through the array and check if a specific element exists. Here is an example that illustrates this using a function.

```
function findInArray(needle, haystack){
    for(var i = 0; i < haystack.length; i++){
        if(haystack[i]==needle){
            return i;
        }
    }

    return -1;
}

var a = [10, 3, 2];

findInArray(a, 3); // equals 1
findInArray(a, 13); // equals -1
```

The above example simply loops through the array and return the index of the array if the element is found. An array can never have a negative index which is why the function above returns a negative value if the loop completes without returning a value i.e. finding the element. However you really don't need to make your own function in JavaScript to search for an element as JavaScript already provides a method for arrays to find the index of elements and it functions in pretty much the same way as the above function would. Meet the `indexOf` function.

```
var pets = ['dog', 'cat', 'hamster', 'bird', 'dog',
'goldfish'];
pets.indexOf('cat'); // returns 1
pets.indexOf('dog'); // returns 0
pets.indexOf('snail'); // returns -1
```

In the above example we see that `indexOf` returns the index of the first occurrence of the element sought. This is why it didn't return index of the last occurrence of 'dog'. To search arrays from the end - we use the `lastIndexOf` function which is a reverse variation of the `indexOf` function.

```
var pets = ['dog', 'cat', 'hamster', 'bird', 'dog',
'goldfish'];
pets.indexOf('dog'); // returns 0
pets.lastIndexOf('dog'); // returns 4
```

The `indexOf` function also takes in a second parameter which is the index from which to start searching from. By default this is zero as the index of function starts to search from the first element in the array. Let's see how this works:

```
var pets = ['dog', 'cat', 'hamster', 'bird', 'dog',
'goldfish'];
pets.indexOf('dog'); // returns 0
pets.indexOf('dog', 2); // returns 4
```

In the above example we told the `indexOf` function to start searching for 'dog' from the index '2' onwards.

Summary

- We touched on JavaScript arrays and the many different functions that allow us to handle arrays.
- We used the sort function to sort arrays.
- We understood that arrays can be concatenated and joined using the concept and join functions.
- We learnt that arrays can be created by using square brackets or creating an Array object with the new keyword.
- We learnt how to add and remove elements from an array.
- We also learnt how arrays can be used in loops and how to loop through an array.

Assignment

Exercise 1
Consider the following array [12, 67,22,12,10,6,8]. Sort the array using a custom made function - do not use the sort function.

Exercise 2

In the following array

```
pets = ['dog', 'cat', 'hamster', 'bird', 'dog',
'goldfish'];
```

Take input from the user and search through the array for the input by the user. When found, remove that element from the array and prompt the user for another input - keep doing this until the user enters a value that is not in the array or until all the array elements have been removed.

Exercise 2

In the following array

```
pets = ['dog', 'cat', 'hamster', 'bird', 'dog',
'goldfish', 'dog', 'bird'];
```

Make a function that removes all the duplicated elements in the above array and creates a new array with the duplicated elements.

Chapter 7: Objects - everything is one!

When talking about Object Oriented development, this is more of a whole new perspective on development than a programmatic approach. While until a decade ago it was seen as an alternative form of development, Object Oriented programming has replaced the age old form of structured development and is now the defect model when it comes to programming. You cannot even lay claim to being a programmer if you don't have a solid foundation in Object oriented Programming techniques and principles.

Overview

We'll touch upon the basic concepts of Object Oriented Programming, what constitutes an object and the benefits of the Object Oriented approach. We will also understand how JavaScript treats Objects and be made aware of the objects we have been using until this time. During this chapter we'll construct a simple Object that illustrates the concepts of Object Oriented programming, note this chapter doesn't aim to be a full-fledged course in Object Oriented Development as the scope of Objected Oriented Development is very vast and cannot be covered in this book. Hence we would be limiting to basic usage and understanding of key concepts.

What's an object?

Literally speaking just about everything in existence is an object. Let's not think programming here, let's think in terms of everything around us. A car is an object, it has specific properties and it has certain functions. Similarly your computer is an object it has certain properties and can perform specific functions. Likewise your cell phone, toaster, sandwich maker, television - etc. In vanilla plain terms, these are all Objects.

How does that translate to programming logic? So far we've been developing using functions and variables. However as in real life it's a fact that all objects perform functions that are directly associated to them. A car has a motor and moves, it isn't used for toasting a sandwich. Likewise you don't tell the weather by talking to a toaster. In programming terms think of an Object as a special block of code that has properties and methods or in this case Variables and functions.

Before you use an Object you need to create one. To create an Object we need to define what is known as a class.

Classes and Objects. What's the difference?

In really blunt terms an Object is an instance of a class. A class can be looked upon as the blueprint upon which an object is made. It is a block of code with functions and properties. When you define a class and then create an

Object from that class the Object gets its own set of properties and methods. Think of it like a manufacturing plant where cars are manufactured. The blueprints to build a car can be assumed to be the class and every individual car that comes out of production is an instance of that class. Don't worry creating Objects won't require you to build a manufacturing plant, but you will need a blueprint i.e. class.

Interestingly we've used a number of Objects and classes all this time without even knowing it. Recall in the last chapter on arrays where we created an array with the following statement:

```
var a = new Array();
```

In the above example `Array` is a JavaScript class that defines an array Object. The `new` keyword creates an instance of the `Array` class. So in the above example the variable `a` is an object of the class `Array` and thus has all the methods and properties of the `Array` class. Just like every car that is built as per a blueprint has its own set of four wheels and engine.

We have also used methods of the array object in our previous chapter. Some methods we used were:

```
var a = new Array();
a.sort();
a.join(',');
a.shift();
```

And not only that but we also made use of a property of the array object namely:

```
var a = new Array();
a.length // length property
```

Methods and properties are defined within the class and can be accessed from the object of the class. And that is what we did in the earlier chapters. Even prior to that we made use of an Object that was already available to us from the very first chapter. The `document` Object:

```
document.write('hi');
```

Note the document object is an object made available in JavaScript, it's not a class but an object and it refers to the page in the browser. The `write` method we used is a method of the document object. Things are starting to get clearer already. We've had a small taste of how we can use Objects and how we've been using Objects for quite a hile now. Let's get down to understanding how they work and how we can make our own Objects.

A Simple Object

Let's make our very first Object. Creating an Object is very simple in JavaScript.

```
var dog = { name:'Fido', breed:'Bulldog', age:2};
```

This looks a bit similar to declaring an array. The main difference is that at its simplest form an Object is technically a non-numerically indexed array. Arrays have only numerical indexes while an Object is not numerically indexed. What looks like indexes are actually called properties? The above example can also be split over several lines - line breaks don't bother objects.

```
var dog = {
        name:'Fido',
        breed:'Bulldog',
        age:2
      };

dog.name; // equals Fido
dog.breed; // equals Bulldog
```

An alternative to creating an Object is by using the JavaScript new keyword to create a new Object.

```
var dog = new Object();
dog.name ='Fido';
dog.breed ='Bulldog';
dog.age = 2;
```

The above code is just the same as the preceding example. Although for simpler objects the preceding example is easier to read and is a preferred way of declaring simple Objects.

Another way to declare Objects is by using what in JavaScript is called an Object constructor or the equivalent of a class in Object Oriented terminology. This is a special declaration which allows you to define a blue print that would define all the objects created from it. For instance in the above examples we declared an object for a single dog. What if we wanted to declare the same for more than one dog? We could explicitly use the same declaration for each and every dog object.

```
var dog1 = { name:'Fido', breed:'Bulldog', age:2};
var dog2 = { name:'Rover', breed:'Wolfhound', age:3};
```

```
var dog3 = { name:'Butch', breed:'Dashdung', age:2};
var dog4 = { name:'Mitch', breed:'Sheepdog', age:2};
var dog5 = { name:'Bowser', breed:'Alsatian', age:2};
```

That is very redundant and highly prone to error. We're creating the same kind of Object here - so it makes sense to use an Object constructor or a class that defines the blueprint of the Object. In this case the class constructor would define the properties namely name, breed and age so we don't have to explicitly define them every time we want to create a dog object. Let's see a demonstration.

```
function dog(name, breed, age) {
    this.name = name;
    this.breed = breed;
    this.age = age;
}

var fido = new dog("Fido", "Bulldog", 3);
var rover = new dog("Rover", "Wolfhound", 2);
```

That is quite a lot happening there, but we can see clearly how much easier it is to create a new dog Object with our object constructor function called dog. This kind of function is called a constructor because it creates and initializes the properties of the Object on 'construction' of it. You have also noticed the use of a new keyword called this. The this keyword is used within the context of an Object. It's used only within the class definition and refers to the Object itself.

It comes into existence when the Object is created. So this.name is the name variable of the Object that was created using the above class constructor. In the above

example you can see the difference between
`this.name` and `name` passed to the constructor function
where `this.name` refers to the objects instance of the
name variable. When creating an Object in this fashion we
can access the properties in the same way as we accessed
the properties of objects created earlier.

```
var fido = new dog("Fido", "Bulldog", 3);
fido.name; //equal 'Fido'
```

With an Object constructor you can create as many objects
as you want of the same type defined by the Objects
constructor.

You can also create an object property even after you have
created an Object. This is done by simply assigning the
new value of the object itself:

```
var fido = new dog("Fido", "Bulldog", 3);
fido.gender = 'male';
```

This is both a boon as well as a bane to JavaScript as while
you have the luxury of editing objects at will, it does get
complicating if your objects can be so easily manipulated.

With Objects as above you can also loop through the
properties using the `for..in` loop as discussed earlier in
arrays. Note that Objects are very much like complex
arrays except that they aren't indexed by numerical values:

```
for(i in fido){

    document.write(i + ':' + fido[i] + '<br />');
}
```

The above example loops through all the properties of the

object and prints out the property name and the value of the property.

Just as with arrays you can also delete a property from an Object using the delete function. However unlike arrays where using the delete function leaves a hole in the array, with objects the delete function removes the property in its entirety from the object itself - no holes here. After deleting a property you cannot refer to it without creating it again.

```
var fido = new dog("Fido", "Bulldog", 3);
delete(fido.name); // now fido has no name
fido.name = 'Butch'; // Fido is now named butch
```

Object do this - adding methods

It's not just properties but you can also assign functions known as methods to objects. A method is declared in the same way for an object as is a property. Let's look at a simple example below:

```
function dog(name, breed, age) {
    this.name = name;
    this.breed = breed;
    this.age = age;
    this.feed = function(food){
        document.write(this.name + ' likes ' + food);
    }
}

var fido = new dog("Fido", "Bulldog", 3);
fido.feed('kibbles'); // prints out 'Fido likes
kibbles'
```

In the above example we declared a method feed, passed it a variable and even invoked it from the Object that was created. The above example also shows how in a function you can refer to the properties of the object using the `this` keyword. At the same time we can also make reference to external objects within the function itself like how we called the document.write method of the document object. Using methods we can also edit the underlying properties of the object as well. Here is an example:

```
function dog(name, breed, age) {
    this.name = name;
    this.breed = breed;
    this.age = age;
    this.addAge = function(years){
        this.age+=years;
    }
}

var fido = new dog("Fido", "Bulldog", 3);
var rover = new dog("Rover", "Sheepdog", 4);

fido.addAge(3);
rover.addAge(5);

fido.age; // equals 6
rover.age; // equals 9
```

We created two objects and made a method that incremented the age property of the individual objects. You can see that both objects have their own distinct properties and methods. Properties and methods are unique to each object created from the same constructor class. Already you can see the versatility we have with regards to using Objects and how Object Oriented development actually works. All associated code and properties are collated within the same Object. Without Objects your code would be a mess of variables and functions and you'd be struggling to try and keep values that were associated with each other together or associated in some way. Consider the following nightmare if we had to do the above without Objects:

```
var fido_name    = 'Fido';
var fido_breed   = 'Bulldog';
var fido_age    = 3;

var rover_name    = 'Rover';
var rover_breed = 'Sheepdog';
var rover_age    = 5;
// Please no more
```

Objects make programming meaningful again

Everything is an object

With JavaScript almost everything is an Object. JavaScript provides a host of default Object types which we use in our day to day programming. When we say everything we mean practically everything. The variables you've been creating, the functions and arrays - everything is an Object and is treated like one. When we say treated like one we mean that all such Objects have their own properties and methods. We didn't define them - because JavaScript has already predefined most of them for us(Isn't that so nice of JavaScript to do that).

Objects native to JavaScript

Just like the `Array` Object as well as the `Object` object JavaScript has defined constructors for numerous Objects. Most of which we've been using all this time such as:

- Numbers
- Strings
- Dates
- Objects
- Arrays
- Functions
- Dates

Some of these objects map to primitive datatypes which we have been using this time. For example let's look at numbers. What does the below code do:

```
var a = 10;
```

If you said it assigns the variable a with the number 10 you're absolutely right. However you can also declare it as a number Object using the JavaScript Number constructor:

```
var a = new Number(10);
```

How this is different from declaring a primitive variable is that when you declare a variable you just declare a variable but when you declare it as an Object of the Number constructor as in the above example you get with it a host of properties and methods. In JavaScript you can treat primitive variables and values as though they were

Objects.

Tip: Use primitive variables, they're faster - use JavaScript Constructors only if you really have to.

Let's look at a few methods and properties you get with a Number Object.

```
var a = new Number(10);
a.NaN(); // Checks if a is a number return true or
false
a.toString; // a is now equal to '10' which is not the
same as 10
```

The NaN method checks if the value is a number or not (NaN = Not A Number). Note this function actually only works if the object is a Number object and checks against the value stored. Alternatively you can use the global function isNaN to check if a variable has a numerical value or not.

```
var a = 10;
a.NaN(); // returns undefined
isNaN(a); // returns false as it is a number
```

Likewise the .toString() function converts the value of the number object to a string value. So we know '10' is not the same as 10 because the latter is a number and the former is a string.

Moving on let's look at the string object. We've used strings in most of our examples and are familiar with the fact that strings are textual data. We've also made use of string related functions in previous chapters. The JavaScript String object will be covered in more detail in the following chapter as will the other main JavaScript objects.

When declaring a string in JavaScript you can do it in one of two ways:

```
var str = 'Hello';
var str = new String('Hello');
```

Both are pretty much the same, however the first method is more faster and efficient. Once you've created a string you get with it a host of methods and properties. For example here is a sampling for some of the properties and methods you get when you use a string.

```
var str = 'Hello';
str.length; // returns 5 the length of the string
str.trim(); // removes trailing whitespaces from both
ends of a string
str.concat(' there'); // concatenates the passed in
string to the string - just like how arrays concat
works
```

We'll discuss more on the various string methods and properties in the following chapter.

Summary

- We touched upon the basics of Object oriented programming.
- Everything in JavaScript is an Object.
- Objects differ from arrays such that they do not have numerical indexes.

- Objects are created from an Object Constructor function.
- Objects can have methods and properties.
- Primitive Data Types in JavaScript are infact Objects.

Assignment

Exercise 1

Create a Person Class with the following attributes:

- First Name
- Last Name
- Age
- Address
- City

Create 10 different unique Person objects and store them in an array. Make another class call it Detective. This class would have at least one function called `find_person_by_name`. This function should take as parameter the first name of a person and return from the array of persons the person object with the name.

Once done make another function that takes a number as parameter and checks for persons who are of a younger age than the number passed and returns the person object.

Chapter 8: The String Object

JavaScript strings are more than just textual data. When you create a string in JavaScript you get a host of properties and methods through which to interact with the string and manipulate it. A thorough knowledge of what the string object holds in JavaScript would help you through the most fundamental programming tasks saving you the time in coding functions that would otherwise be already handled with available methods from the JavaScript string Object.

Overview

We'll discuss the JavaScript string object and go over the various properties and methods available for use by the string object. We'll also understand the implications of the string Objects methods and go over a few real world examples that would illustrate their usage.

All strings are objects

Strings are as you already know, textual data. They can contain alphabets, numbers, operators, accented characters etc. Strings are always enclosed in double or single quotes. When a string contains a single or double quote it is normally escaped with a backslash to prevent JavaScript from assuming that the quote within the string is the enclosing quote. Strings are created in JavaScript just like any other object.

```
var str = 'This is a String';
var str = new String('This is also a string');
```

In the above example we've created strings in one of two ways, by implicitly declaring a variable with a string value and by creating an instance of the String Object. Both ways result in getting a string Object with a number of methods and properties. Let's look at some of the properties and methods that come with the string Object.

How long, and other facts about my string

The string object gives us a few properties to work with. The most commonly used property will be the length property. This as its name infers, returns the length of the string. The length property works just like how the length property works for arrays i.e. with arrays it refers to the number of elements in the array.

```
var str = 'This is a String';
str.length; // equals 16 - note that empty spaces are
also regarded as a string

var str = ' ';
str.length; // equals 1 - empty spaces are also counted

var str = '';
str.length; // equals zero - an empty string is well
empty..
```

On its own the length property can be used to tell if a string is empty or not, but its most commonly used in tandem with either a for loop or other methods used to search or extract from a string. Strings exhibit similar characteristics to arrays in some ways. For example the individual characters in a string can be referred to by an index in the same way as the individual elements of an array would be referred to.

```
var str = 'This is a String';
str[0]; // equals 'T'
str[1]; // equals 'h'
```

As in the above example a string can be taken apart pretty much like an array. Let's use the length property in a simple loop here:

```
var str = 'This is a String';
for(var i = 0; i< str.length; i++){
    document.write(str[i] + '<br/>');
}
```

We've just printed out all the letters in the string on different lines. Just like arrays, the starting index for strings is also zero and this is why running a string through a loop is the same as running an array through a loop.

Searching/slicing - what can you do with a string

Just like other objects strings also have a host of methods that allow you to manipulate and work with the string as you require. This is particularly useful if you would require validating any kind of string input, checking for occurrence of any specific keywords etc. While down the line you'll be introduced to libraries that make the process alot simpler to use its important to be acquainted with the basic native functions that JavaScript offers you with regards to objects. This is because by making use of native JavaScript functions your code will be much more efficient which makes for a better user experience.

If its native to JavaScript it's your best bet

Strings share a lot of similar functions with Arrays. For example we had a look at the `indexOf` function in the chapter of arrays. With arrays this function would return the index of first occurrence of the element passed to it in the array. With strings we have the same function that does pretty much exactly the same thing.

```
var s = "Macaroni and Cheese";
s.indexOf('Cheese');// returns 13
```

You can search for the occurrence of a string within a string and it would return the numeric index of the first occurrence of the string being searched. Think of this as a fundamental search feature. In case the string is not found it returns a negative value.

Note: This function is case sensitive

```
var s = "Macaroni and Cheese";
s.indexOf('Cheese');// returns 13
s.indexOf('CHEESE');// returns -1
```

Its sister counterpart is the `lastIndexOf` function which does pretty much the opposite of `indexOf` and returns the last occurence of the search string passed to it. This is similar to the exact same function used when searching arrays. Just like the `indexOf` method. This function is also case sensitive.

```
var s = "Cheddar Cheese and Gouda Cheese";
s.indexOf('Cheese');// returns 8
s.indexOf('CHEESE');// returns -1

s.lastIndexOf('Cheese');// returns 24
s.lastIndexOf('CHEESE');// returns -1
```

Another commonly used feature is the ability to combine strings. We've already used the plus sign + to concatenate strings in earlier examples.

```
var s = "Cheddar Cheese";
var b = "Fried Onions";
var d = s + ' and ' + b;
d; // equals now 'Cheddar Cheese and Fried Onions'
```

Alternatively you can also use the `concat` method of a string to append as many other strings to it. This is exactly like the `concat` function for arrays. So the above code can be rewritten as below:

```
var s = "Cheddar Cheese";
var b = "Fried Onions";
var d = '';
d.concat(s, ' and ', b);
d; // equals now 'Cheddar Cheese and Fried Onions'
```

Note even with arrays you need to declare a variable as a string in order to use its functions

```
var s = "Cheddar Cheese";
var b = "Fried Onions";
d.concat(s, ' and ', b); // this will not work because
we haven't declared d yet
```

Strings also allow you to manipulate the contents within.
You can change case of all the letters in a string using the
two handy
functions toLowerCase and toUpperCase respectivel
y. One function you'll definitely be using quite often.

```
var s = "Cheddar Cheese";
s.toUpperCase(); // s is now 'CHEDDAR CHEESE'
s.toLowerCase(); // s is now 'cheddar cheese'
```

At times, especially during taking input from users, you'll
want to make sure any data inputted doesn't have any
trailing empty spaces with it. It's ugly to look at and can
cause issues when you wish to sort out string data. Also if
let's assume you're taking in a password and someone
accidentally adds in a few extra spaces too many(it can
happen!), you might end up with a user frustrated that his
password doesn't work because he doesn't recall having
entered any spaces. (Spaces don't make for good
passwords anyway). JavaScript provides
the trim function which trims out any extra trailing or
preceding white spaces.

```
var name = " George Glass   ";
s.trim(); // s is now 'George Glass'
```

Strings in Splits

Remember with arrays we have a `join` function that would technically glue all the elements of the array with a delimiter giving you a string. Strings on the other hand provide an antithesis to that function i.e. the `split` function. Instead of joining thing, the `split` function breaks up a string into an array of sub strings based upon a delimiter to break the string apart. Works like the `join` function for arrays only in reverse.

```
var s = "Cheese,Onions,Pickles,Tomatos";
s.split(',');
s;// equals ['Cheese','Onions','Pickles','Tomatos']

var s = "Dogs and Cats and Mice";
s.split(' and ');
s;// equals ['Dogs','Cats','Mice']
```

Please note that even with the `split` function, the delimiter searched for is case sensitive. By default all string functions are case sensitive.

```
var s = "Cheese and Onions and Tomatos";
s.split(' And ');
s;// equals ["Cheese and Onions and Tomatos"]
```

Search - Regular Expressions Oh My

At this point we would like to introduce a very powerful feature of JavaScript with regards to search for strings. At times when you need to make a search, your queries would be more complex than just looking for a case sensitive occurrence of a substring in a string. What you wish to make sure that an email is a valid email? You could search for the occurrence of the @ symbol - but how can you be sure there aren't any other wrong symbols, and how can you check to make sure it's in the correct format? You'll need to use a lot of nested if statements to pull this one off. And what if you need to check if a phone number entered is valid, or a social security number. Obviously looking for the first and last occurrences wouldn't work here.

Enter the regular expression. Regular expressions are a special sequence of characters that are used to form a search pattern. They can be pretty confusing at first but are very powerful if done right. With regular expressions you define a pattern to search for using a mix of characters. In regular expressions different characters and operators have different implications in forming the pattern.

Regular expressions are declared by either creating an explicit RegExp Object in JavaScript or by declaring the pattern itself between two backslashes / /.

Here is a simple example of a regular expression that does a very simple search.

```
var s = 'Cheese and Onions';
var r = /cheese/i;    // our regular expression
```

We've declared a simple regular expression. On its own it doesn't do much but when we use it with a method that takes in a regular expression i.e. the search method for strings.

```
var s = 'Some Cheese and Onions';
var r = /cheese/i;    // our regular expression
s.search(r); // returns 5
```

The regular expression above is composed of two elements - within the backslashes is the string to be searched. At the end the letter i is used as a 'modifier'. The letter i when used after the backslash stand for case insensitive search so the regular expression when used in a search would return occurrences irrespective of the case they were in. Much more effective than using a mess of if statements!

Also it's not just text that we use between the backslashes for search. Remember we can also write up patterns using special characters to create a search pattern. Let's look at a few simple patterns we can make with regular expressions.

The square brackets [] when used within the backslashes, means to search for any character within the brackets.

```
var r = /[ce]/i;    // our regular expression
```

The above regular expression would match all the occurrences of c and e upper or lower case when used in a search operation. Let's use the regular expressions in another useful function that you'll be using a lot namely the replace function. The replace function takes two parameters the first is a string or a regular expression to search for and the second parameter is a string to replace the matched value with.

```
var s = 'Cheese and Onions';
var r = /cheese/i;    // our regular expression

s.replace(r, 'Thyme'); // r is now 'Thyme and Onions'
```

```
var s = 'Cheese and Onions';
var r = /[ce]/i;     // our regular expression
s.replace(r, 'x'); // s is now `xheese and Onions`
```

This should make sense but in the above example with the
square brackets only the first occurrence of c was
replaced. This is because by default the regular expression
only matched the first occurrence. If we want to match all
occurrences we'll have to make use of a new modifier i.e.
the g modifier. g is the global modifier and matches the
pattern to all possible occurences in the string applied.

Note modifiers can work together

```
var s = 'Cheese and Onions';
var r = /[ce]/g;     // our regular expression
s.replace(r, 'x'); // s is now `Chxxsx and Onions`

var s = 'Cheese and Onions';
var r = /[ce]/ig;    // our regular expression
s.replace(r, 'x'); // s is now `Xhxxsx and Onions`

var s = 'Cheese and Onions';
var r = /[ce]/gi;    // our regular expression
s.replace(r, 'x'); // s is now `Xhxxsx and Onions`
```

Regular expressions are a very complex topic in their own
right and covering even the basic would warrant the use of
an entire book to say the least. We've touched very
sparingly on regular expressions but already you can see
the possibilities and how versatile a search can be made
with the help of regular expressions.

Another interesting function that can be considered for
making searches is the match function. The function as

its name states searches the string and returns the possible match(s) if any. This function differs from search that the `search` function only returns the index of the first occurrence.

```
var s = 'Some Cheese, cheeses and Onions';
var r = /cheese/i;      // our regular expression
s.match(r); // returns ["Cheese"]

var s = 'Some Cheese, cheeses and Onions';
var r = /cheese/gi;     // our regular expression
s.match(r); // returns ["Cheese", "cheese"]
```

How about slicing and dicing some strings?

We've used a few native functions of strings to search through them and make replacements based upon search strings as well as regular expressions. Aside that you can also splice and slice strings like a professional sushi chef.

JavaScript provides the `substring` and the `substr` function. Both function the same way with a few subtle differences. They take two parameters, first the index of the string where to start the extraction, the second parameter is optional. With `substr` it takes in the length of the string to extract. With `substring` it takes in the next index till where to extract. If the second parameter is omitted the entire length of the string from the index is extracted.

```
var s = "Cheese and onions pizza";
s.substring(0, 1); // returns C
s.substr(0, 1); // returns C
```

```
s.substring(2, 4); // returns ees
s.substr(2, 4); // returns eese
```

With the `substring` function if the second value passed in is less than the first value the values are switched as you cannot have the second index to extract to less than the index to extract from.

```
var s = "Cheese and onions pizza";
s.substring(7, 5) == s.substring(5, 7);
```

These functions when used in conjunction with the search functions as well as regular expressions can help in developing complex string manipulation based applications.

Summary

- We know that strings can be created explicitly or by assigning a string value to a variable
- Strings are similar to arrays as they have indexes and share similar functions.
- Strings can also be searched using regular expressions.
- Regular expressions are sequential characters which help to define a search pattern for use with string functions.
- The substring and subrt functions are used to extract parts of a string based upon starting indexes and length / ending indexes.

Assignment

Exercise 1

Create a function that searches and filters a string for a set of nasty words namely the words - stupid, mean, revolting. Have the words replaced with asterisks leaving only the first letter.

Exercise 2

Create a function that validates an email address and doesn't accept any address from 'gmail.com' and 'yahoo.com'.

Chapter 9: The Date Object

One of the most useful objects you can create and use with JavaScript is the `Date` object. This is practically used in every single application there is out there. Getting to know the date isn't any more about just knowing what day it is today as you will soon learn.

Overview

In this chapter we will touch upon the `Date` Object as well as creating and instantiating one. We'll understand how JavaScript works with dates and the many available functions the Date Object provides us. During the course of the chapter we'll understand practical situations where the Date object can be used as well as clarify subtle issues that may cause confusion if overlooked.

The Date - we're talking calendars here!

JavaScript provides a built in Date class constructor to create a date object, and no these are not the edible types and they don't involve romantic rendezvous. The date object is used to work with dates and times. It also allows you to work with and manipulate the constituents of a date i.e. years, months, days, seconds, minutes, hours and milliseconds. The date object carries with it a huge drove of methods and properties. Dates on their own are a special type of data in programming, they are specially represented as a datatype in all databases and almost every programming language has provisions for handling dates.

Creating a Date Object is very easy, you just have to make an explicit declaration of the date object:

```
var dt = new Date();
```

The above dt variable is a date Object. If you were to output this using document.write you would get the current date - time to the nearest millisecond and even the time zone you're in. Something like:

Wed Dec 31 2014 11:49:31 GMT+0400 (Arabian Standard Time)

The Date Object takes the current date as it is set on the machine you're running the site from. Remember that JavaScript is a client sided language meaning it runs in the browser hence the date taken would be the date as set in your computer. To try it out, just change the date and time in your computer and run the code again - you'll see it reflects the date on your computer.

This is the simplest way to get the current date, you can always output the current date on your website this way in just two lines of JavaScript code. Alternatively you can also initialize the Date Object with a custom date of your choice. To initialize the date object you can do it in one of three different ways.

```
var dt = new Date(milliseconds);
var dt = new Date(date_as_a_string);
```

```
var dt = new Date(year, month, day, hours, minutes,
seconds, milliseconds);
```

Let's take a look at them one by one. The first instantiation
method takes as a parameter a number representing the
number of milliseconds that have passed since Zero time.

Zero time refers to 01 January, 1970 00:00:00 (UTC), all
programs us this date as a focal point from which all dates
are calculated from in terms of milliseconds. One day is
equal to 86,400,000 milliseconds.

The number of milliseconds passed from Zero time is
added to get the new date when instantiating the date
object. If a negative value is used we get a date before
Zero time.

```
var dt = new Date(86400000); // dt is now equal to 02
January, 1970 00:00:00 UTC assuming your PC's timezone
is set to UTC
var dt = new Date(-86400000); // dt is now equal to 31
December, 1969 00:00:00 UTC assuming your PC's timezone
is set to UTC
```

Calculating the number of milliseconds from the first
moment in 1970 isn't exactly how human beings think in
terms of dates. Alternatively you can also pass a date as a
string to the Date Object in order to instantiate it. Be
warned though that the string passed must be a valid date
and adhere to a specific format.

```
var dt = new Date('Wed Dec 31 2014 11:49:31 GMT+0400
(Arabian Standard Time)'); // dt is now equal to Wed
Dec 31 2014 11:49:31 GMT+0400 (Arabian Standard Time)
var dt = new Date('December 31 2014 10:30'); // this
also works dt is now equal to Wed Dec 31 2014 10:30:00
```

```
var dt = new Date('December-31-2014 10:30'); // this
also works dt is now equal to Wed Dec 31 2014 10:30:00

var dt = new Date('December 31 2014'); // this also
works dt is now equal to Wed Dec 31 2014 00:00:00
var dt = new Date('31 Dec 2014'); // this also works dt
is now equal to Wed Dec 31 2014 00:00:00

var dt = new Date('31st Dec 2014'); // this doesn't
work
var dt = new Date('31/12/2014'); // even this won't
work
```

As you can see JavaScript is smart enough to tell the date from however you pass it. However there are limitations as to how much can JavaScript decipher a date from a string. The date has to be of a format that JavaScript can understand, while this will work well most of the time - during development you might want to have a bit more control on setting up the date in JavaScript. For that you can declare a date Object by explicitly passing in the years, months, days, hours, minutes and seconds as parameters when instantiating the Date object.

```
var dt = new Date(2012,11,31,10,30,30,0); // dt is now
equal to Wed Dec 31 2012 10:30:30 GMT+0400 (Arabian
Standard Time)
```

In the above example we passed in the year, month, day, hour, minute, seconds and milliseconds respectively to construct a date.

Note that the first month is represented by 0 in JavaScript so January would be 0 and December would be 11

Also understand that most of the variables are optional. If

you omit the hours days and minutes it would use a default value instead.

```
var dt = new Date(2012,11,31); // dt is now equal to
Wed Dec 31 2012 00:00:00 GMT+0400 (Arabian Standard
Time)
var dt = new Date(2012,11); // dt is now equal to Wed
Dec 1 2012 00:00:00 GMT+0400 (Arabian Standard Time)
```

Incidentally if you were to use for the month a number greater than 11 the date would be incremented the number of months over 11.

```
var dt = new Date(2012,11,31); // dt is now equal to
Dec 31 2012 00:00:00 GMT+0400 (Arabian Standard Time)
var dt = new Date(2012,12,31); // dt is now equal to
January 31 2013 - 12 is December plus one more month
var dt = new Date(2012,13,10); // dt is now equal to
February 10 2013 - 13 is December plus two more months
in the next year
var dt = new Date(2012,13,40); // dt is now equal to
March 2013 - 13 is December plus two more months in the
next year
```

This is very helpful when you would want to create a specific date without having to worry too much about getting the right format plus it's really useful if you need to run dates through a loop.

Dates are displayed automatically thanks to the toString method. By default when you create a date object you've essentially created an Object, yet when you print it out using document.write it flawlessly prints out as a string as we've seen it. Otherwise if you create a custom Object and try to print that out as it is it would only print out Object. This is on account of the `toString` method, whenever a date Object has to be treated as a string, JavaScript automatically makes a call to this method.

```
var dt = new Date(2012,11,31);
document.write(dt) == document.write(dt.toString()); //
Both are the same
```

Dates constitute of?

JavaScripts Date Object gives you a myriad of methods to manipulate dates. While we've seen how you can create a custom Date Object with a string, set of parameters and milliseconds. It's what you can do after you've gotten a Date Object that really brings the power of this Object to the fore. We need to understand and obviously know that a Date is composed of a Year, Month and Day. Since JavaScript Date Objects also take time into consideration a Date also thus constitutes hours, minutes, seconds and milliseconds. We have a host of functions that allow us to retrieve and alter any component of a date object. This is very useful especially if you wish to do date comparisons.

```
var dt = new Date(2012,11,31, 10, 30, 20); // It's the
last day of 2012 and the world hasnt ended yet! Woo
Hoo!
dt.getFullYear(); // Returns 2012
dt.getMonth(); // Returns 11, the month of the date!
dt.getDate(); //  Returns 31 - the date of the month
dt.getDay(); // We get 1 which is a Monday - Sunday is
0, Monday is 1 all the way down to Saturday which is 6
dt.getHours(); // Returns 10
dt.getMinutes(); // Returns 30 minutes
```

```
dt.getSeconds(); // self explanatory
dt.getMilliseconds(); // self explanatory
```

JavaScript also provides a `getTime` method which gets the time in milliseconds of the assigned date from Zero time. This is very useful if you wish to check if one date is later or earlier than another, especially if you wish to sort an array based on dates.

Note in all the above methods, the details retrieved are with respect to the time zone on your computer. In addition to the above methods, JavaScript also provides similar methods which get the same details only with respect to UTC, taking into account the time zone on your PC. They're aptly named as below:

```
var dt = new Date(2012,11,31, 10, 30, 20); // A few
minutes to a few hours can totally change a date
dt.getUTCFullYear(); // Returns the year adjusted for
UTC
dt.getUTCMonth(); // Returns the month adjusted for UTC
dt.getUTCDate(); //  Returns the day adjusted for UTC
dt.getUTCDay(); // Returns the day of the week adjusted
for UTC
dt.getUTCHours(); // Returns the hours adjusted for UTC
dt.getUTCMinutes(); // Returns minutes adjusted for UTC
dt.getUTCSeconds(); // self explanatory again
dt.getUTCMilliseconds(); // self explanatory
dt.getUTCDate(); // Returns the whole date adjusted for
UTC - the UTC adjusted equivalent of getDate()
```

It's important to take the time zone difference into consideration when working with dates. You have to be aware of the users' time zone and when he may have made a transaction. Normally dates are stored based on Universal Standard Time and then converted to match the time zone of the user for viewing in a web page.

You may have noticed a common pattern in all the above methods is that they all start with the prefix `get`. Objects have properties and rather than access properties directly, it is common Object Oriented Programming practice to have simple functions which get the values of these individual properties. They are called getter functions and are normally named as such with `get` prefixed to the name of the property they return. Just like you have getter functions you also have setter functions which set individual properties of an object. They follow a similar naming convention and thus are prefixed with the word `set`. So all of the above functions have their setter alternatives which take one variable and adjust the corresponding property.

```
dt.setFullYear(2013); // Takes the year and sets it
dt.setMonth(2); // Takes a number 0 to 11 corresponding
to the month
dt.setDate(23); //  Take a number between 1 to 31 and
sets the date of the month
dt.setHours(12); // Takes a number between 0 to 23 and
sets the hour
dt.setMinutes(54); // Any number between 0 to 59
dt.setSeconds(45); // self explanatory again
dt.setMilliseconds(); // self explanatory
```

Plus the very same functions also come with their UTC counterparts which set the corresponding date component adjusted for UTC.

```
dt.setUTCFullYear(2013); // Takes the year and sets it
adjusting for UTC
dt.setUTCMonth(2); // Takes a number 0 to 11
corresponding to the month adjusting for UTC
```

```
dt.setUTCDate(23); //  Take a number between 1 to 31
and sets the date of the month adjusting for UTC
dt.setUTCHours(12); // Takes a number between 0 to 23
and sets the hour adjusting for UTC
dt.setUTCMinutes(54); // Any number between 0 to 59
adjusting for UTC
dt.setUTCSeconds(45); // self explanatory again
dt.setUTCMilliseconds(); // self explanatory
```

Just like we have the date function `getTime` which
returns the number of milliseconds from the current time
and date till zero time, we also have the corresponding
setTime function which takes a numeric parameter
corresponding to the number of milliseconds since the zero
time and sets the date accordingly. This is just like passing
the number of milliseconds to a date Object when creating
it to initialize it.

```
dt.setTime(86400000); // dt is now equal to 02 January,
1970 00:00:00 UTC assuming your PC's timezone is set to
UTC
dt.setTime(-86400000); // dt is now equal to 31
December, 1969 00:00:00 UTC assuming your PC's timezone
is set to UTC
```

While these may seem like an awful lot of functions to
remember, they're quite easy to remember and each
function acts upon one component of the date element.

Getting down and personal with dates

In addition to the above functions JavaScript also provides
a set of functions that deal with more than just a single

component of the Date Object.

We've seen the different functions for getting dates and time constituents for both the current systems time and also for UTC time in relation to the current systems time. In addition to this you can also find out the UTC offset from the current systems time by usage of the `getTimezoneOffset` function. This would return the time difference from the local time and UTC time in minutes as a positive or negative integer depending on what timezone you are in.

```
var dt = new Date(); // initialize a date object
dt.getTimezoneOffset(); // returns 240 since local time
is UTC +4 hours hence 4 times 60 is 240
```

This can be very useful when trying to build a time zone convertor in JavaScript.

While speaking of conversions, we must know that JavaScript relies heavily on the zero time as a placeholder around which time comparisons are done.

The `parse` function in JavaScript takes a string date and returns in milliseconds the difference between the parsed date and Zero Time. This function is pretty much the same as instantiating a date Object with a string and then calling the getTime function.

Only this is a class function i.e. you don't create an Object to use this function, it's called directly from the Date class.

```
var dt = new Date('31 March, 2014');

dt.getTime() == Date.parse('31 March, 2014');
```

So far we've played around with dates and their constituent elements as well as converted strings to dates. We know that to output a date we can simply out put the date Object. The Date object provides a few more functions that are helpful when it comes to outputting the date besides the toString function.

```
var dt = new Date();
dt.toString(); // Thu Jan 01 2015 17:07:17 GMT+0400
(GST)
dt.toDateString(); // Thu Jan 01 2015
dt.toUTCString(); // Thu, 01 Jan 2015 13:05:59 GMT
dt.toTimeString(); // 17:05:56 GMT+0400 (GST)
```

Along with the toString function you can also output the date partially using the toDateString or just the time portion of the date using the toTimeString function. And don't forget there's also a UTC equivalent of these functions to print the UTC equivalent.

Summary

We know that JavaScript provides a complex date object for manipulating dates. Dates can be instantiated in four different ways. Zero time refers to January 1st 1970 midnight. Dates in JavaScript are stored as milliseconds in reference to zero time. The individual components of a date can be retrieved and set using native Date objects getter and setter functions

Assignment

Exercise 1

Make a function that takes as a parameter an array of dates and sorts them.

Exercise 2

Write a class with a method that takes as parameter a string of the format d/m/y where d refers to the day, m refers to the month and y the year. The method should return the current date formatted as the string passed so if the following string is passed m, d Y the date should be January,10 2015.

Chapter 10: The Document is an Object

While we're on the subject of Object oriented programming, lets also know that with working on web pages - object orientation goes a very long way. Its not just variables and dates that are considered or referred to as objects but also just about everything on the HTML page including the page itself is regarded as an object and like all objects have their own methods and properties which can be accessed and manipulated.

Overview

In this chapter we'll learn about the Document Object Model which defines the different elements that make up a webpage and how each element is an object. We'll also learn that every element on the page is a node including the page itself as well as the different attributes and methods available for interacting with them.

Everything is an Object

The HTML DOM or Document Object Model is a w3 standard for defining and accessing content of a webpage i.e. document. The HTML DOM is standard conventional interface which defines all elements as objects as well as the properties inherent to each element as well as the methods and events available for each element.

Every element in a webpage including the webpage itself is referred to as a node. The nodes are arranged in a tree like structure with the document node as the root node with the other nodes following in for example:

```
<html>
  <head></head>
  <body></body>
</html>
```

The first node in the document node is the `html` node which branches out into the `head` element node and the `body` element node respectively and so forth.

When a web page is rendered, a Document Object Model of the page is created with each and every element loading as a node on the tree. This is a very important way to understand the DOM in order to be able to interact and manipulate it which we would do so using the many methods available to us from the DOM.

Every element on the page including the page itself is an object of the class node. The node is the base class which defines every element in the page as well as the page itself. And on account of this almost all the objects have similar methods and properties as well as their own specialized properties.

Let's start off by creating a basic HTML page which we would use for the rest of this exercise. You can put all the

JavaScript code either in a `script` tag in the head of the page or in an external `.js` file and link to that file as an external script.

```html
<html>
  <head>
    <title>Hello World</title>
  </head>
  <body>
    <h1 id="heading">The Page</h1>
    <p id="sub" class="base">This is some text on the
page</p>
    <table class="base">
      <tr>
        <td>Item</td>
        <td>A</td>
      </tr>
      <tr>
        <td>Item</td>
        <td>B</td>
      </tr>
    </table>

    <ul name="list">
      <li>Element 1</li>
      <li>Element 2</li>
      <li>Element 3</li>
    </ul>
  </body>
</html>
```

We'll use this html page for the rest of this chapter with small variations. To understand the different functions available for the DOM, we'll make use of them and see their practical implications.

Console console?

Before we proceed we need to be acquainted with a small tool that you will definitely be using a lot when you start real development. In browsers firefox and Chrome as well as Opera you have the option of inspecting elements. Right click on any part of the screen and you should have a menu option to inspect the element. This actually opens up a panel to the bottom or side of the browser which shows the entire current page as it is with the element inspected highlighted.

Give it a try and you'll understand how it works.

While this alone is very useful, you'll notice that the panel which has opened has a number of useful tabs. We won't be looking at all of the tabs but you'll definitely have a script tab, an HTML tab and a console tab as well. We'll be interested in the console tab. The panels on modern browsers allow a simple function called `console.log` that allows you to output an element or just about anything to this console tab. If you were to output an HTML element using document. Write you would only output HTML and it would be rendered on screen, however using console.log you can output just about anything to the console tab and really refine development in the process.

Try the console.log function - let's output a simple bit of text:

```
console.log('This is some text');
```

Run the page and you'll see while nothing appears on the page, in the inspect > console tab the text has been displayed. Let's try and pass an array to the console.log function.

```
console.log([1,2,3,4,5]);
```

You see that the output in the console tab, you can click on it and actually view the contents of the array. To the side you can also view in the DOM panel a list of all the methods and properties native to the array. Some of those methods and properties would look very familiar as we've covered them. Already you can see the usefulness of this tool. We would be using this extensively during the course of this chapter.

Note that this feature is a development tool when your site is production ready you would not want to have console.log functions lying around in your deployed code.

Let's get back to our page. By default we already have a document object to work with. The document object refers to the page that has been loaded. Incidentally the document object is a child object of another object namely the window object which refers to your browser. The browser can also be controlled via JavaScript and is also referred as an object. We'll look at what devious schemes we can do with the browser in a later chapter.

Since the document is the core node of any web page all of the methods we would be using would be inherent to the document object.

The first function we'll be using is `getElementById`. This function does as its name sake and selects the element based on the id of the element. It takes in a string which is the id of the element. Let's pick the h1 element in the above page.

```
var el = document.getElementById('heading');
console.log(el);
```

We assigned the node retrieved by the getElementById function to a variable and outputted it in the console. You should be able to see the element in your console panel - click on it and you'll even see the content of the node itself.

Now that you know how to capture an element let's see what you can do with it. We'll manipulate the elements properties in the next example. How about changing the content of the h1 node? All nodes carry with them an `innerHTML` property which refers to the entire HTML contained within the node. Let's use this to change the heading using JavaScript.

```
var el = document.getElementById('heading');
el.innerHTML = 'New Heading';
document.getElementById('heading').innerHTML = 'Another heading'; // this works as well
```

You've now manipulated your first element. What if you try to get an element with a wrong id?

```
var el = document.getElementById('head_ing');
el; // this equals undefined
el.innerHTML = 'New Heading'; // throws an error
document.getElementById('head_ing').innerHTML =
'Another heading'; // will throw an error
```

As a good practice it's important to check to make sure if an element actually exists prior to manipulating it. This is because since JavaScript is an interpreted language, the minute an error is encountered the script would halt and won't proceed beyond the point of error. Checking for an undefined object is simple:

```
var el = document.getElementById('head_ing');
if(el){
  el.innerHTML = 'New Heading';
}
```

The if statement is very versatile, if the element would be null or false it would be evaluated as false, and if the variable has any kind of value that isn't null or undefined or false the condition would evaluate to true.

Note in order to check a variable for a true or false value you must have declared the variable beforehand.

There are a number of methods available in native JavaScript to retrieve elements on the page. We've learnt how to retrieve an element by searching for an element with a specific id, how about searching for an element based on another set of parameters:

```
var a = document.getElementsByClassName('base');
var a = document.getElementsByTagName('li');
var a = document.getElementsByName('list');
```

The above methods of the `document` object retrieve elements based upon
the `class`, `tag` and `name` respectively. All the above functions return an array of possible elements. So

the `getElementsByTagName` function returns an array of all the `li` tags in the entire document. You can output using the console function whatever has been retrieved using this manner.

Just as the document object has methods and properties so do all the nodes have their own properties. We've checked the `innerHTML` property of the `h1` node already in the above example.

Note - the getElementById only returns a single element and not an array. If you have more than one element on your page with the same ID – that is really bad HTML you have there!

Repeat everything is an Object again

What interesting to note is that just as the `document` model has its own set of properties and methods, so do the elements on the page. Since all the elements including the document itself inherits from the Node Object - they all share a lot of similar functions yet at the same time some elements have their own set of functions and properties.

For example an `a` element will have an `href` attribute which obviously a `p` or `table` would not. And likewise some elements are displayed as `block` while some are `inline` by default. This is better covered when you would study HTML and CSS, so we would be covering the methods available to elements as well.

Let's add the following HTML to our page

```html
<div id="parent1" class="one">
  <p class="pink"></p>
  <p class="pink" name="para"></p>
  <div id="red"></div>
</div>
<p class="pink"></p>
```

In the above HTML you have some p elements and a div element nested within the div element with the class one. The nested elements are the child elements of the parent element which is the div classed one. We could select the pink classed elements above using the document functions as below:

```javascript
var pink_els = document.getElementsByClassName('pink');
```

And incidentally we can also retrieve them via the parent elements.

```javascript
var p = document.getElementById('parent1');
p.getElementsByClassName('pink');
```

The above example returns an array of elements just like the previous example, but if you inspect it in the console by outputting it, you'll notice that the previous example returned three elements in the array while this example returned only two. The reason being is that these retrieval elements work in relation to the object invoking them. The document object contains every HTML element hence,
thegetElementsByClassName or getElementsBy

`TagName` search through all the contained elements. When used with an element, it searches through all the child nodes or elements of that single parent element.

You can use this array of elements as any other array like using it in a loop:

```
var p = document.getElementById('parent1');
var a = p.getElementsByClassName('pink');

for(var i = 0; i< a.length; i++){
  console.log(a[i]); // outputs one element at a time
  a[i].innerHTML = i; // replaces the contents of the
class `pink` elements with the respective index
}
```

Let' s manipulate

Now that you know how the DOM actually works, how you can retrieve individual or groups of elements from the document or from within elements itself lets move on to some methods and properties that will allow us to do a bit of manipulation.

Before we do this lets add some css to our HTML. You can do this by either creating an external css file or linking to it in a `link` tag or by adding css in a style tag block in the head of the document. Let's make a few styles here:

```
.pink{
  color:DeepPink;
}

.red{
```

```
  color:Red;
}

.blue{
  color:Blue;
}

.one{
  padding:10px;
}
```

We'll start by changing some basic attributes. Initially we used the innerHTML property to completely change the contained HTML of any node that could be selected. All elements have a getAttribute, method that returns the attribute passed to it. So if I have an element I can always use this to find out about its individual attributes:

```
var el = document.getElementById('parent1');
el.getAttribute('class'); //returns one
```

Not bad but what if we don't know what the element is and need to check for an attribute that doesn't even exist. Like only links have href attributes. We have another method that allows us to check if an element has an attribute aptly named hasAttribute:

```
var el = document.getElementById('parent1');
el.hasAttribute('href'); //returns false
```

That is all said and done let's combine the two functions and do a bit of manipulation here. Let's change the class of the parent1 element here, for this say hello to the setAttribute.

```
var el = document.getElementById('parent1');
```

```
if(el.hasAttribute('class')){
  el.setAttribute('class', 'blue');
}
```

Whoa that really changed some color there. But wait - we seemed to have lost the padding that was with the original class. That is because we've overwritten the attribute. If we want to simply append the classname we would use the `getAttribute` function to retrieve the existing class before making the change.

```
var el = document.getElementById('parent1');
if(el.hasAttribute('class')){
  cls = el.getAttribute('class'); // cls is now one
  el.setAttribute('class', 'blue ' + cls);
}
```

We set the class to have both the `blue` and the `one` class as an appended string. This is a very versatile set of functions that allow us to do pretty much anything with any attribute of any element.

Aside that you don't really need to use the above get and set functions and can directly edit the class by accessing the elements className property.

```
var el = document.getElementById('parent1');
if(el.hasAttribute('class')){
  cls = el.className; // cls is now one
  el.className = 'blue ' + cls;
}
```

The above code works exactly as the code above it. A number of attributes can be accessed in this manner which is common to all elements such as:

```
node.title  // sets or returns the title
```

```
node.title = 'This is title';
node.title; // returns 'This is title'

node.id
node.id = 'parent2';
node.id; //returns parent2
```

The `style` property works a bit differently in that in the
style property refers to an Object which holds all the css
declarations as individual properties. So for example:

```
<div id="text" style="border-top:1px solid #CCC;
color:red"></div>

var el = document.getElementById('text')''
el.style.borderTop;// returns 1px solid #CCC
el.style.color = 'blue'; // changes the color style to
blue
```

It's best to use the `style` property to edit inline styles
instead of the `setAttribute` function as it will
overwrite the entire style attribute.

Traversal Traversal / Add and Remove!

We can select elements, we can manipulate them now -
we've pretty much gained control over the page here.
However so far we have been manipulating with respect to
class names, ids and tag names. Very often you would
need to access elements with reference to their positioning
with other elements in the page. For example you can't
have an id for just about every single element on the page
that seems impractical especially if your page is complex

and filled with a lot of HTML. What if you wanted to select and change the color of elements next to elements of a specific id, or what if you wanted to change the class names of the nth list item in an unordered list? You can only do so much with loops and looping through every single element on the page is highly impractical and will definitely slow down and crash your page.

Here we look at a few methods that allow us to easily traverse the DOM. These methods take full advantage of the tree structure on which the DOM is based that elements can have parent and child elements.

For this example we'll be using the following HTML snippet.

```
<table class="base">
  <tr>
    <td>Item</td>
    <td>A</td>
  </tr>
  <tr>
    <td>Item</td>
    <td>B</td>
  </tr>
</table>

<ul name="list">
  <li>Element 1</li>
  <li>Element 2</li>
  <li>Element 3</li>
</ul>
```

Let's say we want to access the first element in the unordered list. Let's use the `childNodes` property which returns all the child nodes of the element.

```
var el = document.getElementsByName('list')[0];
var ch = el.childNodes;
console.log(ch);
```

We should get an array of three elements but wait, we get
an array of more than that here? What gives you may
wonder. The `childNodes` property returns all the
childNodes and even considers white text and spaces as
nodes - so the indentation spaces those are also treated as
individual nodes. You could rewrite the HTML without
spaces but it would be terrible to read at this point.

```
<ul name="list"><li>Element
1</li><li>Element2</li><li>Element 3</li></ul>
```

That is valid html but not easy to ready for us primitive
humans. Thankfully we have another property that does
exactly the same but gloriously ignores the empty elements
and spaces. Let's hear it for the elements `children`.

```
var el = document.getElementsByName('list')[0];
var ch = el.children;
console.log(ch); // gets all child elements in an array
```

That is awesome, but we still want to access the second
element. We can do this by referencing the second index of
the array of elements.

```
var el = document.getElementsByName('list')[0];
var ch = el.children;
ch[1];
```

However there is an easier way to do that, we'll use
the `firstChild` property here. It returns the first child
element.

```
var ch =
document.getElementsByName('list')[0].firstChild;
console.log(ch); // ????
```

Wait it got an empty string as the first child? The reason is
that like the childNodes property this property also treats
whitespaces as individual element. Technically trimming
out all whitespaces makes for a faster loading page. So use
the same code on the HTML without the spaces and you
should get the first element.

Alternatively we can use
the `firstElementChild` property here as this
conveniently ignores whitespaces and comments. So keep
your easy to read HTML code and use the following
JavaScript:

```
var ch =
document.getElementsByName('list')[0].firstElementChild
;
console.log(ch); // ????
```

But wait how do we get the second element. In this case
we're lookting to get the element next in line to the current
selected firstChild. Note that all elements on the same
level are called siblings, an element which encases other
elements is called a parent element of the encased
elements. And the encased elements are called the child
elements of the parent element. JavaScript provides two
interesting functions to move through sibling elements just
as we've moved to the children element by using
the `firstChild` property.

```
// note use this with space free html
var ch =
```

```
document.getElementsByName('list')[0].firstChild;
ch2 = ch.nextSibling
ch == ch2.previousSibling

// note use this with regular html
var ch =
document.getElementsByName('list')[0].firstElementChild
;
ch2 = ch.nextElementSibling
ch == ch2.previousElementSibling
```

The two functions and their
variations previousSibling, nextSibling move
through the DOM by accessing the adjacent elements on
the same level. We first retrieved the first element after
which we then traversed and moved onto the second
element which was adjacent to the first element.

Let's take these things a bit further - how about if we
wanted to remove the second element. Or maybe add
another element here. We can do that with JavaScript.

```
// note use this with space free html
var list = document.getElementsByName('list')[0];
var ch = list.firstChild;
list.removeChild(ch); // we removed the firstChild
```

The removeChild method takes the actual node to be
removed from the parent element. It's the parent element
making the removal here. Likewise we can add child
Elements similarly using
the appendChildand insertBefore functions.

Before inserting an element you need to create it or use an
existing element. Let's create a new list element and add it
to our list.

```
// note use this with space free html
var list = document.getElementsByName('list')[0];
var li = document.createElement("li");
li.innerHTML = 'This was added';
list.appendChild(li);
list.lastChild; // returns li
```

The `createElement` function of the document model
creates an element based on the tag that has been passed.
Once you have created an element you get all the attributes
and methods that all the elements possess. In the above we
set the innerHTML property of our newly created list item
and we added it to the list using
the `appendChild` method of the list element. This
method is owned by all elements. The
`appendChild` element adds the passed element as the
last child of the parent element, as we have seen with
the `lastChild` property. You can alternatively insert the
element anywhere you like using the
`insertBefore` method. It takes the node to be inserted
as well as the node before which it should be added. So
you can add a node anywhere in the document.

```
// note use this with space free html
var list = document.getElementsByName('list')[0];
var li = document.createElement("li");
li.innerHTML = 'This was added';
list.insertBefore(li, list.lastChild); // added before
the last child element
list.insertBefore(li, list.firstChild); // added before
the first child element
```

Just as with the firstChild, the nextSibling,
previousSibling, lastChild have their corresponding text

node inclusive versions that ignore text as nodes called `nextElementSibling, previousElementSibling` and `lastElementChild` respectively

Using these methods and properties you can really manipulate and wreak havoc (just kidding don't do that though) with the DOM. This gives you an idea of how much power you have with the JavaScript language.

Summary

• The DOM Model is a specification for HTML elements.

• The DOM models all html elements as a tree with parent and child nodes with the document node as the top most node above which is the window object that references the browser.

• Objects can be retrieved by attributes such as id, tag, names and class names.

• Elements can be traverses through using respective methods and properties of each element.

• Parent elements contain child elements and siblings are elements on the same level

Assignment

Exercise 1

Create an array of person objects that have the properties - name, age, description and email. Using the methods learnt in this chapter, using only JavaScript create a table of all the person objects in each row.

Exercise 2

In addition to the above exercise, add another property to the persons called `active` which takes a value of true or false. Set some persons to be active and some not active. Using JavaScript, mark the background colors of table rows with active persons with a green color and inactive persons with a gray color.

Chapter 11: Events - what just happened?

Manipulating the DOM, traversing and playing around with an HTML page seem like a lot of fun. But there is no fun if the end user can't do much interaction here. So far we've tried out examples where all the manipulation was done in code with zero input from the outside world aka the user. This pretty much defeats the purpose of using JavaScript in the first place. But don't fret - JavaScript comes with a highly detailed events model that allows us to code user specific events that are native to all HTML elements. Users do stuff with the mouse and the keyboard and we need to be able to capture all those details and give the user the interactive experience that they so rightly deserve.

Overview

In this chapter we'll take a look at the event model in JavaScript, what events are and how do we code for them. We'll understand the idea of an event Handler and the different events available to us by the DOM and the different types of events.

Events in JavaScript

In laymen's terms an event is something that occurs or just happens without any pre-emotive warning. That click from the users mouse, the form that was just submitted, the browser resizing, the drag - those are all events. JavaScript allows us to register event handlers which are essentially blocks of code to events. This means that an event handler is a block of code that has been registered to be executed whenever an event occurs.

Events take place on elements, and are executed by the user in a myriad of ways.

Before we go further we need to look at the various different events we have in JavaScript and how they are grouped.

Events - Don't Mouse around!

The most basic form of interaction in HTML is the a tag. It's a simple link to a different page or resource. However all DOM elements are able to respond to just about any kind of event. The majority of all events expected would definitely be via the mouse or cursor. Hence all events relative to DOM elements are based on user actions with the mouse.

Let's make a simple example of an event handler here within HTML itself

```
<a href="http://www.yahoo.com" onclick="return
false;">Click</a>
```

Put that in your HTML file and try to click on the link. For
some reason it won't work. If you look at the code you'll
realize that we've added an onclick attribute to the element.
onclick actually corresponds to the users click action, and
the contents of this attribute is pure JavaScript. This bit of
code merely returns the boolean value false. Returning
false to a click handler basically means don't do anything.
And that is what we've done here. Let's modify that a bit

```
<a href="http://www.yahoo.com" onclick="return
confirm('Are you sure?');">Click</a>
```

Run that and now click, you'll get a confirmation, if you
respond with affirmative it redirects because you passed it
a true value, and if you choose the otherwise it doesn't
redirect because you've passed to it false. This is a very
simple way of coding in an event handler. But what if we
needed to do this for more than one link?

```
<a href="http://www.yahoo.com" onclick="return
confirm('Are you sure?');">Click</a>
<a href="http://www.google.com" onclick="return
confirm('Are you sure?');">Click</a>
<a href="http://www.bing.com" onclick="return
confirm('Are you sure?');">Click</a>
```

This is pretty monotonous. What we can do is put our
JavaScript into a function and call that function.

```
function doConfirm(){
  return confirm('Are you sure?');
}
```

```
<a href="http://www.yahoo.com"
onclick="doConfirm()">Click</a>
<a href="http://www.google.com"
onclick="doConfirm()">Click</a>
<a href="http://www.bing.com"
onclick="doConfirm()">Click</a>
```

Much better but again we need to make a call to each function - let's put all the code to handle the even in JavaScript here.

```
var a = document.getElementsByTagName('a');
for(var i = 0; i< a.length; i++){
  a[i].onclick = function(){
    return confirm('Are you sure?');
  }
}

<a href="http://www.yahoo.com">Click</a>
<a href="http://www.google.com">Click</a>
<a href="http://www.bing.com">Click</a>
```

Definitely much better, as you can see we've selected all the a elements and assigned the individual onclick events a function. The HTML is clean and we don't have any intermixing of JavaScript and HTML.

Note: Keep you HTML and JavaScript separate

This is one example using the onclick event. Also understand that it's not just the a link tag that responds to an onclick event. Any element you have can respond to an onclick event. Let's try this with a paragraph and use some css to give the paragraph a background color so we know what we're clicking on.

```
<p id="clickable" style="background-color:yellow">
```

```
You can click on me
</p>

document.getElementById('clickable').onclick =
function(){
  return alert('Hi!');
}
```

Just click on the paragraph and voila you get an alert pop up. This is all well and interesting, however consider the following example JavaScript with the same html:

```
document.getElementById('clickable').onclick =
function(){
  this.style.backgroundColor = 'red';
}
```

Click the paragraph and you see the color changes. What just happened and how? In the above JavaScript we've introduced the `this` keyword. We used it when working with classes to declare class properties and methods and it refers to the current object itself. In this case it was a reference to the `clickable` paragraph object and made reference to its style. The event handler merely changed the color of the objects background on click. Already you can see the possibilities with the events in JavaScript.

Let's take a look at another event namely the `dblclick` event. This captures a double click from the mouse. Let's modify the above JavaScript so on click the background color changes to red and on double click it changes to yellow.

```
var el = document.getElementById('clickable');
el.onclick = function(){
  this.style.backgroundColor = 'red';
```

```
}
el.ondblclick = function(){
  this.style.backgroundColor = 'yellow';
}
```

You can click like crazy now and see the colors change. Just as we have the click and double click events we also have a host of other mouse events that can be used such as:

Event	description
element.onmousedown	The moment you press a mouse button over an element
element.onmouseenter	Just when the mouse cursor enters an element
element.onmouseleave	Just as the cursor moves out of an element
element.onmousemove	When the mouse moves while it is over an element
element.onmouseover	Like the mouseenter event but also occurs if you move the mouse over any child elements of the element
element.onmouseout	Like mouseleave - only it also works if you move out of any child element of the element
element.onmouseup	After you click just as you leave the mouse button on an element

The onmouseenter and the onmouseover seem pretty much the same but have subtle differences. We'll demonstrate it with a demo here. Chalk up the following

HTML.

```html
<div id="counter">0</div>

<div id="moveover" style="background-color:red;">
MOVE OVER
<p style="background-color:black;"> A paragraph </p>
</div>
<div id="moveenter" style="background-color:red;">
MOVE ENTER
<p style="background-color:black;"> A paragraph</p>
</div>
```

```javascript
var el = document.getElementById('moveover');
var a = 0;
var b = 0;
el.onmouseover = function(){
document.getElementById('counter').innerHTML=a+1;
}
var el1 = document.getElementById('moveenter');
el1.onmouseenter = function(){
document.getElementById('counter').innerHTML+=a+1;
}
```

In the above example you'll notice that if you move your cursor over the MOVE ENTER div it only increments the counter once, however if you move into the MOVE OVER div every time you move over the div as well as the contained black paragraph you'll notice the counter is incremented i.e the event is fired. This is a subtle difference between the two events and you'll need to be careful in handling the right event here to avoid any possible mistakes.

Similar to these are the onmouseleave and the onmouseout event except that onmouseleave is fired when the mouse leaves the element itself, while the `onmouseout` event is fired when the mouse moves out of the element or any child element. We can rewrite the above JavaScript to demonstrate this:

```
var el = document.getElementById('moveover');
var a = 0;
var b = 0;

var counter = document.getElementById('counter');
el.onmouseover = function(){
  counter.innerHTML = a+1;
}
el.onmouseleave = function(){
  counter.innerHTML = a-1;
}

var el1 = document.getElementById('moveenter');
el1.onmouseenter = function(){
  counter.innerHTML+=a+1;
}
el.onmouseout = function(){
  counter.innerHTML = a-1;
}
```

Run the code and you can see that if you leave the MOVE OVER div it decrements the counter just once you've moved, however if you move out of the MOVE ENTER div it decrements the number of times you move in and out of the div and its child element the paragraph.

This is a very simple example to demonstrate the differences between the mouse events and how they are fired.

Every button fires!

It's not just the mouse whose events are captured but also the keyboard. Any of the keys you press on your keyboard can have a specific event handler registered to it. There are three events associated with the keyboard namely:

1.onkeydown
2.onkeypress
3.onkeyup

These three events occur every time you tap a key on the keyboard and the occur in the exact same order as above. When you press a key the first event to be fired is the keydown event, once the key has been pressed the keypress event is fired at the end when you release the key - the keyup event has been fired.

As a matter of convention use the keydown event as it fires for all keys in all browsers

The keyboard functions obviously for sake of ease of usage aren't like the mouse events where you can just interact with anything as you can't really maneuver the page much with just a keyboard except for form elements. So we'll try this with an example form element. Set up the following html and JavaScript respectively.

```
<input id="foo" />
<div id="counter"></div>

var el = document.getElementById('foo');
el.onkeydown = function(){
  counter = document.getElementById('counter');
```

```
  counter.innerHTML = this.value.length
}
```

Run that and you have a text box. Type in it and you
should see a counter increment and decrement as you type.
All form elements have a property called value which
returns the value that has been entered into the element.
Every time you make a keypress the event is fired which
triggers the handler, which in turn fills the counter with the
string length of the text entered in the text field.

What if you needed to be specific with respect to the keys
that are entered? Let's assume you want the counter to
only fire if the spacebar is passed, there has to be a way to
track which key is pressed. Luckily in JavaScript using the
event handlers, this is as simple as passing a parameter to
your handler. So far we haven't passed any parameters
explicitly to our parameters, but for every event handler an
event object is passed to all our events. Let's declare a
variable for the first parameter passed to our event handler.

```
var el = document.getElementById('foo');
el.onkeydown = function(e){
  counter = document.getElementById('counter');
  if(e.keyCode==32){
    counter.innerHTML = this.value.length
  }
}
```

Run that code and type, we see that only when the space
bar is pressed does the even handler take action. There is a
lot that seems to be going on in the above code. We're
using the variable e to refer to the event object which is
automatically passed to the event handler. This event

Object carries information about the event that has just occurred and one of the properties of the event is the keyCode property. This contains the key code value for the key that was pressed. These are unicode values that represent each key on the keyboard. You can make a simple script to see what the unicode values of each key can be using simple JavaScript. Let's modify the above example here:

```
var el = document.getElementById('foo');
el.onkeydown = function(e){
  counter = document.getElementById('counter');
  counter.innerHTML = e.keyCode;
}
```

Typing in the input box now shows the code for every key you clicked in. This is awesome but what if we want to tell what key the code represents. Luckily the String Object comes with it a method called String.fromCharCode that can convert the unicode value to its corresponding key. Let's modify the above example again:

```
var el = document.getElementById('foo');
el.onkeydown = function(e){
  counter = document.getElementById('counter');
  code = e.keyCode;
  counter.innerHTML = String.fromCharCode(code);
}
```

Go ahead and try it out - the counter is now populated with the key you must have pressed. You might notice that it works fine for basic alphanumerical characters but not for other keys such as the enter key, escape and some characters.

This is because unicode as a specification isn't meant for just keyboards. Your best bet would be to use the original character codes in your code if you want to compare for a character that has been entered.

If the form fits

One of the most common areas in JavaScript where you would be inundated with event handling is perhaps on forms. We mentioned at the start of the book one of the pitfalls with having no client sided scripting to check for validations on your forms. Here we take a look at the events that are exclusive to form elements and how they can be used to create compelling event handlers.

Forms are one of the most basic and main forms of interaction with the user and websites. It's the primary way to receive data from the user to be used on the server.

We'll start off by getting acquainted with four basic events of forms
namely `onblur`, `onfocus`, `onchange` and `onsubmit`
.

The `onfocus` event actually fires when you've focused on a form element. Focus means when you've selected or your keyboard/mouse is 'focused' on that element.
The `onblur` event fires is the focus shifts, like if you use the tab key to move from an element to another, as you 'leave' the element, the elements `onblur` event is

triggered and the next element where you 'land' on its `onfocus` event is triggered.

Let's make a simple form here to work with:

```html
<form id="theForm" method="post">
<p>
  <label>Name</label><br/>
  <input type="text" id="name" name="name" />
</p>
<p>
  <label>Age</label><br/>
  <input type="text" id="age" name="age" />
</p>
<p>
  <label>Gender</label><br/>
  <select id="gender" name="gender">
    <option>Please choose Gender</option>
    <option value="male">Male</option>
    <option value="female">Female</option>
  </select>
</p>
<p>
  <label>About</label><br/>
  <textarea id="about" name="about"></textarea>
</p>
<p>
  <input type="submit" value="Save"/>
</p>
</form>
```

Plus lets add some css rules that we can use:

```css
.error{
  border:1px solid red;
}
.busy{
  border:1px solid green;
}
```

The form takes in some basic information. We need to add

some validation to this form. Let's start with making sure that the user doesn't leave the name field blank to begin with. This can be done a number of ways but for the sake of demonstrating the `onblur` field we'll do this so whenever he tries to shift away from the name field if its empty, the name field gets a red border around it to showcase that something is wrong.

```
var el = document.getElementById('name');
el.onblur = function(){
  if(this.value == ''){
    this.className = 'error';
  }else{
    this.className = '';
  }
}
```

Run the code in the browser, just focus on the name field and without entering anything just shift focus by clicking somewhere else or using the tab key. You'll see that the text field now has a border applied to it. This is a visual cue to the user that something is wrong. Go back to the text field and enter a value and then move away from the field, you'll see the border is now gone. This is pretty awesome in itself. The above code is very simple, it runs whenever focus is shifted away from the `name` field element.

Let's tidy this up a bit, you see that when you shift away from the field and it's empty, a red border is applied to the field. When you shift back, the border is still there and stays there unless you add in text and shift away again. Let's add another event handler so when you focus on the name field, it removes any excess border.

```
var el = document.getElementById('name');
el.onblur = function(){
  if(this.value == ''){
    this.className = 'error';
  }else{
    this.className = '';
  }
}

el.onfocus = function(){
  this.className = '';
}
```

Run the code and you can see the subtle difference. focus back to the name field after you leave it whilst its empty and error class is removed. This demonstrates how onfocus and onblur work.

The onchange event is mostly used with select elements and is triggered when the value of the element has changed. It can be used also with other form elements but its most effectively used with the select element. Let's put an annoying popup whenever the gender field is changed and outputs a silly message.

Note - please avoid using too many popups else your users will hate you for it

Add the following JavaScript to the above:

```
var gender = document.getElementById('gender');
gender.onchange = function(){
  alert('You are '+this.value);
}
```

Run that code and just change the value in the select field, you'll be greeted with a silly popup that tells you what you've outputted. The `onchange` event is triggered only when the value of the element is changed.

Now that we understand how those work, there is one more main event that we have yet to cover with forms. The onsubmit event. Forms like all elements are also a node, and likewise they have their own specific methods and properties and likewise their own events.
The `onsubmit` event is triggered when a form is submitted. Normally this is where you would add an event handler that would check to make sure the form is submitting with valid details. With the above code, you do give the user visual cues but the form will still submit. Lets work on the form a bit and make sure that it doesn't submit unless you have at least a name entered. For this we'll work on the `onsubmit` handler.

```
var frm = document.getElementById('theForm');
frm.onsubmit = function(){
  if(document.getElementById('name').value == ''){
    alert('The form is not valid, name cannot be
empty!');

  }
}
```

Run that code without entering the name and booyah! You get an error message in a popup. But wait a second, you click ok on the pop up and the form still submitted - why is that you may wonder? That is because in order to halt the normal action, you need to return a boolean false in the event handler. This ensures that the form is not submitted.

So make the following adjustment:

```
var frm = document.getElementById('theForm');
frm.onsubmit = function(){
  if(document.getElementById('name').value == ''){
    alert('The form is not valid, name cannot be
empty!');
    return false;

  }else{
    return true;
  }
}
```

And you're good to go, now the form doesn't submit if there is an empty name field.

Note the else statement in the above example is not really needed and it can function just as well without it.

Summary

- We've learnt how JavaScript events work
- Events can be captured and code can be assigned to events in what are called event handlers.
- Event handlers are passed an event object by default which represents the event that has occurred and contains data about the event.
- Keyboard events register a corresponding keycode value in the event Object where each keycode is a Unicode value representation the key that was pressed.

- Forms have their own set of events.
- OnBlur and OnFocus refer to the events of losing/getting focus respectively.
- The form's onsubmit even allows us to run code prior to submitting the form eg: validation code.

Assignments

Exercise 1

In the above form example, write a set of onblur and onfocus event handlers for the age field that checks if the age entered is a positive integer.

Exercise 2

Refactor the functions above, put them all in a dedicated Object for validation which can be reused. use the object for validating on blur/onfocus handlers as well as in the onsubmit handler. This is so you do not repeat the same code in the submit handler as you would have written in the other individual fields event handlers.

Chapter 12: Beyond the HTML - accessing the Browser?

So far we've understood a number of key concepts regarding nodes. We've seen detailed examples that explain how all nodes are objects with their own methods and properties. We also understood the DOM structure, the tree like structure on the basis of which web pages were constructed. That every node would branch out into further nodes akin to HTML tags nesting other HTML tags and so forth. Aside this we also understood that the document model although it is at the root of the page is also container by the window Object i.e. in this case the browser. The browser itself can also be referenced just like the DOM, giving us unprecedented control on the user experience that goes beyond the HTML on the page.

Overview

We will learn about the BOM i.e. the Browser Object Model, and our focus will be on the window object as well as the practical implications of its methods. We'll learn how to redirect users as well as understand how to set cookies to store user specific information for later access. Plus we'll go over a few examples that illustrate the many different methods and features of the window object.

The Window Object - yes your browser is in our control!

The BOM, of Browser Object Model is pretty much like the browsers version of the DOM. However different browsers tend to define the 'BOM' with a few variations unlike the DOM which is defined by the worldwide web consortium. So there really isn't a standardized BOM as of yet. However we would be covering all the common methods available through the window Object which allows us to access, control, manipulate and technically hold the browser for ransom (scratch that part on holding the browser for ransom).

The `Window` object just like all other objects functions as a node, although it is pretty much the actual root here, it contains the document which represents the page. Since we're pretty clear on what the document model has to offer let's take a look at the basic methods that the browser provides us through the `Window` object.

To start with the document itself is a property of the window Object to begin with. If we were to look at the following bit of code:

```
document.write('Hello there!');        // this is the
same..
window.document.write('Hello there!'); // ..as this
```

We can see that `window.document` is just the same as writing `document`. Since `document` is a global variable, it's safe to assume that all global variables are accessible by the window Object and so are global functions.

```
g = 10; // This is globally declared
window.g == g; // g can be accessed from window as its
a global variable
```

It's clear that the window Object has access to variables and functions in the global scope. This allows us to control the browser based solely on code.

Can I get curtains for my window?

The window object can be used to get the actual size of the browser in pixels.

```
window.innerHeight; // returns the height of the
browser window
window.innerWidth;  // returns the width of the browser
window
```

As we stated that because the BOM is not standardized, eaelier versions of Internet Explorer had their own different methods to attain the same result here. Try this little exercise out, write down the following code.

```
document.write('Height is ' + window.innerHeight +
'px<br/>');
document.write('Width is ' + window.innerWidth +
'px<br/>');
```

Run the code and it should return a set of values, now resize your browser and refresh it, You should see a different set of values corresponding to the new size fo your browser screen. This is exceptionally useful in cases where you might want to hide or show certain elements based upon the size of your browser screen. Earlier websites would use JavaScript to adjust content for mobile sized screens, however this practice has been replaced with the advent of HTML5 and CSS3. Nevertheless this is still a useful feature.

Opening/Referencing Browser windows with JavaScript

This is probably one of the most irritating yet common uses of the `window` object. You've probably seen the ability to open popups on many websites. This is made possible using the `window.open` method of the`window` object.

While pop ups are frowned upon and most users would prefer to block pop ups, there are a number of situations where you might require a pop up window. Banks even today make use of JavaScript based window popups to show virtual keyboards online where instead of typing out using your keyboard you click on a virtual keyboard on the screen to enter your credentials. Plus a window once it has been opened using JavaScript can also be referenced later on in code.

Let's make a simple example here. Type out the following html and JavaScript. As good convention we'll keep the

JavaScript and html separate as we've been doing all this time now.

```
<a href="#" id="open-window">Open a Window</a><br/>
<a href="#" id="close-window">Close the Window</a>
```

We'll set the open a window link to open the yahoo website in a popup window.

```
var op = document.getElementById('open-window');
op.onclick = function(){
  window.open('http://www.yahoo.com');
}
```

Run the code and click the Open a window link. It should open the yahoo site in a popup window. This is pretty basic stuff and you might be wondering why bother if this can be replicated witha simple target attribute in the link. The `window.open` method takes a number of parameters that allow you to actually manipulate the window opened. The `window.open` method takes the following parameters:

```
window.open(url, name, option, replace);
```

Let's go over the parameters, the url is understood as the url to open in the window. However the name attribute refers to one of the following values if passed:

- '_blank' if this is passed the URL is loaded in a new window, this is the default action
- '_parent', if you've worked with frames before you'll understand that the parent frame here refers to the owning frame which contains the current page, in our example we don't have frame so this shouldn't

really apply.

• '_self' - this means to load the url into the current page, in which case this isn't a popup. The url would be loaded in this very same window

• any name, this would be a name that we can use to reference the window in any later bit of code

Let's add another link here that opens the google page in the same window that would open.

```
<a href="#" id="open-window">Open a Window</a><br/>
<a href="#" id="open-google">Open Google</a><br/>
<a href="#" id="close-window">Close the Window</a>
```

Let's make some modifications to the JavaScript

```JavaScript
var op = document.getElementById('open-window');
op.onclick = function(){
  window.open('http://www.yahoo.com', 'basic');
}

var op = document.getElementById('open-google');
op.onclick = function(){
  window.open('http://www.google.com', 'basic');
}
```

Run that code and click on the first link, it open a window just like it did before, now click on the open google link. Suprisingly, we don't get another window instead the google website opens up in the same original window. If you look at the code above we assigned a name, 'basic' to the window when we opened it up. This can be any name you want it be, however by doing so we can now reference the same window object in our code. This allows us to manipulate a window object from another page, provided those object was created from the same page code though.

Alternatively, the window.open method also returns a window object that we can use just like it was another object, and assign it to a variable. Let's modify the code above, change the names of the links a bit.

```
var op = document.getElementById('open-window');
op.onclick = function(){
  wn = window.open('', 'basic');
}

var opg = document.getElementById('open-google');
opg.onclick = function(){
  wn.open('http://www.google.com', 'basic');
}
```

In the above code, we made the first link open a blank window, and assigned the returned window object to a variable wn. Then we opened the google site the same window using that objects open property. With a reference to the newly created window, we can do more than just open a site in it, let's add another link on the page and some more JavaScript:

```
<a href="#" id="open-window">Open a Window</a><br/>
<a href="#" id="open-google">Open Google</a><br/>
<a href="#" id="write-stuff">Write Stuff</a><br/>
<a href="#" id="close-window">Close the Window</a>

var op = document.getElementById('open-window');
op.onclick = function(){
  wn = window.open('', 'basic');
}

var opw = document.getElementById('write-stuff');
opw.onclick = function(){
```

```
  wn.document.write('Hello there', 'basic');
}

var opg = document.getElementById('open-google');
opg.onclick = function(){
  wn.open('http://www.google.com', 'basic');
}
```

Run the code, open the blank window, then click on the write link, amazingly you can write text in your newly created window from code in the original window.

Note this example also illustrates that the document object is a node of the window object

Closing an opened window is just as simple. Just make a call to window.close.

```
var opc = document.getElementById('close-window');
opg.onclick = function(){
  wn.close();
}
```

Add the above code and the close button link closes the newly created window. The window.open function also provides a number of ways to modify the window that has been opened up. You can set its size, show and hide toolbars and buttons on the browser etc. Fot these modifications we'll look at the third parameter passed to the window.open function. This parameter takes a sting of comma separated settings that define the required modifications to the newly opened window.

The following is a list of examples that outline the different settings.

```
window.open('', '', 'height=300'); //blank window opens
with a height of 300 pixels
window.open('', '', 'left=100'); //blank window opens
100 pixels to the left of the screen
window.open('', '', 'location=no'); //Hide the location
bar, take yes to show it - not supported by all
browsers
window.open('', '', 'menubar=no'); //Hide the menubar ,
take yes to show it - not supported by all browsers
window.open('', '', 'resizable=no'); //Allows/
disallows window from being resizable - not supported
by all browsers
window.open('', '', 'scrollbars=no'); //Hide the
scollbars, take yes to show it - not supported by all
browsers
window.open('', '', 'status=no'); //Hide the status
bar, take yes to show it
window.open('', '', 'width=300'); //blank window opens
with a width of 300 pixels
window.open('', '', 'width=300, height:400, left=150,
location=no'); //blank window opens with a width of 300
pixels, 400 pixels height, 150 pixels to the left and
no location bar
```

As you can see that using the `window.open` function
you can do more than just open urls in a different window,
going as far as to customize the nature and even
positioning of the window.

Note: Even though this is all cool and fun, in real life
settings, window pop ups are frowned upon and should be
used only sparingly.

Browser specific functions -lets navigate

All modern browsers provide another object namely called the `navigator` object. This is a basic object which technically refers directly to the browser. While the window object referred to the actual instance of an open browser window, the navigator object instead refers to the browser itself. Both the window and navigator object are used hand in hand to create a rich fulfilling interactive experience for the user.

Here is a basic example of one of the `navigator` objects functions:

```
navigator.language;// This returns the language of the
browser
document.write('This browser speaks ' +
navigator.language);
```

Assuming you have Us English as the default language set on your browser you should get something like:

```
This browser speaks en-US
```

Aside that the navigator object also allows you to retrieve information about the browser such as what browser it is, the user agent which is more details about the browser and what operating system its running on etc.

```
document.write('This browsers user agent is ' +
navigator.userAgent);
document.write('<br/>This browser is ' +
navigator.appName);
```

If you run the above code you should see two lines with

distinctive information - something like:

```
This browsers user agent is Mozilla/5.0 (X11; Ubuntu;
Linux x86_64; rv:34.0) Gecko/20100101 Firefox/34.0
This browser is Netscape
```

This should show you the difference in values
that `.useAgent` and `.appName` return. While you may
find it hard to understand where these functions can even
be used, during the course of development you may run
into situations where you might require to know
beforehand the kind of browser as well as the operating
system run by your users example for an online survey, or
if you wish to allow/disallow a download link if it supports
the users operating system.

Where are you man! GeoLocationing

This is perhaps one of the more common and fascinating
uses of the navigator object. The
navigators' `geolocation` property provides functions
that return the actual geolocation of the user. This actually
requires the user to give approval prior to getting the users
position. Using this you can pin point to a very fair degree
of accuracy the location of the user. This information can
be used to populate a map or store coordinates. Let's try a
simple example here.

```
function writePos(position){
  document.write("Latitude: " +
position.coords.latitude + '<br/>');
  document.write("Longitude: " +
```

```
position.coords.longitude);
}

navigator.geolocation.getCurrentPosition(writePos);
```

Run the above code, your browser should ask you whether or not you want to share your location. Allow the browser and you should see written above the coordinates as noted in the writePos function. Now what is going on here, we'll have to deconstruct the code a bit.

The `navigator.geolocation` property is a geolocation object which provides a function `getCurrentPosition`, this function takes as a parameter a function to which it passes a position object which contains its own set of properties, one of which we've sued is the `coords` property. This in turn holds the respective `latitude` and `longitude` values of the user browser.

These latitude and longitude values can be used to show the users location on a map.

Using such information you can tailor an application to get location specific details which could be of interest to the user.

Let's use Google Maps api to show the location on a map - this is really quick stuff here. Let's rewrite the above code so we not only read the coordinates but also see a small map.

```
function writePos(position){

  var map_url =
```

```
"http://maps.googleapis.com/maps/api/staticmap?center="
+position.coords.latitude + "," +
position.coords.longitude+"&zoom=12&size=550x400&sensor
=false";

   document.write("Latitude: " +
position.coords.latitude + '<br/>');
   document.write("Longitude: " +
position.coords.longitude);

   document.write('<br/><img src="' + map_url + '" />');
}

navigator.geolocation.getCurrentPosition(writePos);
```

Run that code, in the above we've used google maps api
which returns an image based upon the coordinates passed
to it. You should now see a map that shows you your
location, well at least close enough to freak you out!

Redirect users at will

Another oft used property provided by
the window document object is location. This isn't
geolocation, just refers to the web url in your browser.
The location object on its own provides a series of
functions and attributes that can be set or retrieved. We'll
go over a few of them.

```
// assuming we're on
http://www.somesite.com/page/1?v=12
window.location.hostname; // returns the hostname -
based on the above example www.somesite.com
window.location.href // returns or sets the entire url
window.location.pathname; // returns or sets the
```

```
pathname or as above /page/1
window.location.search; // returns or sets the
querystring i.e. ?v=12
```

The location object allows you to deconstruct and access/modify many parts of the url in the browser. Let's use for a simple example the `href` property which is the most commonly used to redirect users from a webpage. Write up the following code:

```
<a href="#" id="link-to-yahoo">Go To Yahoo</a>

var a = document.getElementById('link-to-yahoo');

a.onclick = function(){
  window.location.href = 'http://www.yahoo.com';
}
```

Run the code and click on the link, you'll see we can now redirect to yahoo. Think of a situation where you want to redirect to a location inputted by the user for an example, or to a link that is constructed in real-time. Plus at times you would want to redirect based upon the users input i.e. to an error page, or let's say the user doesn't permit you to access his location, you could use the above to redirect to an error page on your site.

Go back in time - or History

One more very useful function of the browser is the ability to go back in history, the browsers history that is. Sure you can say that you can always use the back button on your browser. But that defeats the whole purpose of making your web page user friendly in the first place. At times you might want a reference to the last page the user has been on, or you might want to check where the user has come to your page from. We'll make use of the `window.history` object. Let's make a link that sends us back to a page in our history.

```
<a href="#" id="link-to-back">Go Back</a>

var a = document.getElementById('link-to-back');

a.onclick = function(){
  window.location.href = window.history.back();
}
```

Open a few pages and then navigate to your code page. Run it and click on the link, you'll see that you've been sent back to the previous page you were on. Alternatively the `history` object also provides a `forward` method which moves you one page ahead if you came to the current page by clicking back. At times you would want to have a go back link on your web pages, it's much better than having the user figure out that the only way out is to use the back button on his browser, in which case its highly unlikely that he'd ever want to come back again!

Do you want a cookie?

We're not talking about what goes well with milk and cream, a cookie is a file created by a website on your browser which holds data. Whenever you use a website you're making a request to a server which sends back html. However there is no way for the website to actually identify you as a unique user. Cookies help in identifying the user by storing information about the user on the users browser. For example a website where you enter your name on entry, if we didn't use cookies you would have to enter your name every time you'd visit the site during a session, however when the name is stored by the website in a cookie, it identifies you and knows your name.

Cookies are stored as pairs of values and attributes separated by semicolons eg:

```
'name=Bob; Age=32;'
```

Cookies can also have an expiry date attached to them, this allows the browser to clear out old cookies as well as keep cookies with data stored for a copious amount of time. Example:

```
'name=Bob; Age=32; expires=Thu, 1 Feb 2015 12:00:00 UTC'
```

By default cookies are deleted when the browser is closed, only cookies that have an expiry date remain until the date.

Creating a cookie is simple just using `document.cookie`.

```
document.cookie = 'name=Bob; Age=32; expires=Thu, 1 Feb 2015 12:00:00 UTC';
```

A cookie can also be changed, you just need to change the properties that were passed to the original cookie:

```
document.cookie = 'name=Jimmy; Age=16; expires=Fri, 2
Feb 2015 12:00:00 UTC';
```

Deleting cookies is simple, just pass in a passed expiry
date and the cookie would be deleted.

```
document.cookie = 'name=; Age=; expires=Thu, 01 Jan
1970 00:00:00 UTC';
```

To access a cookie, you can use
the `document.cookie` property to retrieve all cookies
that have been stored. Note retrieving a cookie will return
the above string as a string, you would need to use a bit of
string manipulation to retrieve individual values from a
cookie here.

Note that it is important that if you use cookies on your
website, that you make it known to the user that your
website uses cookies.

Summary

- We learnt that the navigator object is used to return
  browser specific information
- We understood how geolocation works and how to
  display coordinates of the current user.
- We also understood the location object and how to
  redirect users as well as deconstruct the url in the
  browser.
- We were introduced to cookies and understood
  how cookies work as well as how to set, retrieve and

destroy - cookies.

Assignment

Exercise 1

Create a script that asks for the users name using a prompt.
The script should set a cookie and store it. When the user
comes back to the same page, the script must check the
cookie to make sure it exists, if it does, output a
friendly `Hello` and address the name of the user.

Exercise 2

In the above script create a link that when clicked deletes
the cookie.

Exercise 3

Create a script that takes the location of the user and stores
it in a cookie. Code it so when the user visits the page
again, and does not allow divulging his location, making
the script check for the location in the cookie and output it.
At the same time allow whenever the user allows the script
to access his location to overwrite the cookie.

Chapter 13: JS in action - Form validation

We've come a long way since the start of this chapter, now it's time to actually put our skills to some practical usage here. We'll try to implement whatever we've learnt in a full-fledged basic form which will illustrate whatever we've learnt throughout the course of this book. This application is meant to be a starting point which would give you an idea of how to program in a real live situation.

Overview

We will construct a basic front end application that takes in user information and stores them in an array of objects. We'll work out a scheme to store objects and arrays. Using this application we'll also allow the user to add and delete elements. For this we will also make use of validation techniques to test and make sure that input is validated using JavaScript. Errors would be displayed on the form illustrating the ability to manipulate the DOM and individual elements.

Our basic form

We'll make a simple form that takes basic input about the

user such as his name, date of birth, address and email address. We want to make sure that the user enters all of this information correctly. For the date of birth we'll use three select inputs instead of having the user enter the date manually in a text box for ease of usage. Let's create our form so far:

```
<form id="theForm">
  <p>
    <label for="name">Full Name</label><br />
    <input id="name" name="name" />
  </p>
  <p>
    <label for="dob">Date of Birth</label><br />
    <select id="dob_day" name="dob[day]"></select>
    <select id="dob_month" name="dob[month]"></select>
    <select id="dob_year" name="dob[year]"></select>
  </p>
  <p>
    <label for="address">Address</label><br />
    <input id="address" name="address" />
  </p>
  <p>
    <label for="city">City</label><br />
    <input id="city" name="city" />
  </p>
  <p>
    <input type="submit" />
  </p>
</form>
```

This is pretty simple stuff so far, now remember we need to create more than one user and store them as an array of users. To start with let's create a user object in JavaScript that would represent one user.

```
function user(name) {
  this.name = name;
```

```
   this.dob = '';
   this.address = '';
   this.city = '';
}
```

The above piece of code is a very basic user object declaration. It just takes and assigns a name value. For now this is standard fare. Let's code it so on submission of the form we create a user object:

```
function user(name) {
   this.name = name;
   this.dob = '';
   this.address = '';
   this.city = '';
}

var frm = document.getElementById('theForm');
frm.onsubmit = function(){
   user1 = new
user(document.getElementById('name').value);
}
```

Not bad but this doesn't seem to do much, remember we need to create an array of users here - so let's create another object to represent the array. We can use an array directly as you can declare a variable in the global scope however it is best practice to make use of an object and restrict yourselves to using that object instead of manipulating variables at will.

Our user list object will hold an array, we'll have just one user list here and that will hold an array that stores all the created objects.

```
function list(){
   this.list = [];
```

```
}

var theList = new list();
```

This is pretty swell, but how do we add users to the list?
Let's create a set of functions that will help us here. These
functions should add a user to the list, remove a user from
the list based on the index, and get a user from the list
based upon his index. Let's add some functions here:

```
function list(){

  this.list = [];

  this.add = function(elem){
    this.list.push(elem);
  }

  this.remove = function(index){
    this.list.splice(index, 1);
  }

  this.get = function(index){
    this.list[index];
  }
}
```

This is more comprehensive, now we have a list object that
can add, remove and get an element from an array. The
add functions makes use of the push method we learnt of
earlier, while the remove method makes use of the splice
method to remove an element.

Now that we have that set up let's code so our form now
adds our entered user (at least with his name) to the user
list array.

```
var frm = document.getElementById('theForm');
```

```
var theList = new list();

frm.onsubmit = function(){
  theList.add(new
user(document.getElementById('name').value));
  return false;
}
```

Run your code and you should have a form, keep on entering names and submit the form. It doesn't seem like anything is happening. We need to show all the users that are being created in the list should we? Let's adjust the html a bit so we have an unordered list of users that have been inputted. This list will be appended with a new entry every time we submit the form. Add the following under your form

```
<ul id="ourList">
</ul>
```

Now we need to add an `li` element for every user that is added. We can do this on submitting the form but it makes more sense to let the logic for handling how to show the listed elements to the list. For this we'll add a few functions:

```
function user(name) {
  this.name = name;
  this.dob = '';
  this.address = '';
  this.city = '';

  this.getHTML = function(){
    html = this.name;
    return html;
  }
```

```
}


function list(){

  this.list = [];
  this.html = ''

  this.add = function(elem){
    this.list.push(elem);
    this.buildHTML(elem);
  }

  this.buildHTML = function(elem){
    html = '<li>';
    html = html + elem.getHTML();
    html = html + '</li>';
    this.html += html;
  }

  this.getHTML = function(){
    return this.html;
  }


  this.remove = function(index){
    this.list.splice(index, 1);
  }

  this.get = function(index){
    this.list[index];
  }
}
```

In the user object we added a function that returns an
HTML representation of the object in this case just the
name. In the list object we have added an HTML property
that stores html that would represent the entire list. In this
we have also added a function that adds to the html

property a list item whenever a list item is added to the list. Plus a function that returns the entire list in html format. Let's adjust our submit handler so we also alter the unordered list with the list of added users.

```
var frm = document.getElementById('theForm');
var theList = new list();
var ul =  document.getElementById('ourList');

frm.onsubmit = function(){
  theList.add(new
user(document.getElementById('name').value));
  ul.innerHTML = theList.getHTML();
  return false;
}
```

Run the code and you can see that with all awesomeness, the list is updated as and as you type and submit the form.

Complex Dates

So far our form is just taking in the name, but we have with it on the form a number of other fields that belong to the user object. While the city and address fields are no issues at all, the date field is a little tricky here. We're taking for the date three fields i.e. day, month and year but need to store a valid date object for every user. This is where that date manipulation will come in handy here. Let's start off by populating the select inputs with some options. Now for the options we can do this by typing in some HTML but we'll do it using JavaScript. To start with, let's use a loop to populate the day variable with days from

1 to 31. Add the following code to your JavaScript.

```
day = document.getElementById('dob_day');

for(i=1; i<=31; i++){
   op = document.createElement('option');
   op.setAttribute('value', i);
   op.innerHTML = i;
   day.appendChild(op);
}
```

Run the code and very cleverly you'll see that the day select has been populated with options. Let's also add the months to the month field. We'll loop through the value 0 to 11 - remember months start with a zero index in JavaScript, because we need to store the date as a date object. Add the following JavaScript:

```
month = document.getElementById('dob_month');

for(i=0; i<=11; i++){
   op = document.createElement('option');
   op.setAttribute('value', i);
   var d = new Date('', (i+1));
   month.appendChild(op);
}
```

That works pretty fine, now for the year, we want to list out at least 100 years before the current year. For this we'll run a loop and loop through numbers from the current year upto 100 years earlier. We'll get the current year using the Date Object.

```
var d = new Date();
var current_year = d.getFullYear();

year = document.getElementById('dob_year');
```

```
for(i=current_year; i>=(current_year - 100); i--){
  op = document.createElement('option');
  op.setAttribute('value', i);
  op.innerHTML = i;
  year.appendChild(op);
}
```

Awesome, now you have populated the required fields, let's rewrite the user object a bit so we have a few methods that set the properties:

```
function user(name) {
  this.name = name;
  this.dob = '';
  this.address = '';
  this.city = '';

  this.getName = function(){
    return this.name;
  }

  this.getCity = function(){
    return this.city;
  }

  this.getAddress = function(){
    return this.address;
  }

  this.getDob = function(){
    return this.dob;
  }

  this.setName = function(name){
    this.name = name;
  }

  this.setCity = function(city){
    this.city = city;
  }
```

```
this.setAddress = function(address){
    this.address = address;
}

this.setDob = function(day, month, year){
    this.dob = new Date(day, month, year);
}

this.getHTML = function(){
    html = '<p style="padding:5px; border:1px solid
#ccc;">'
    html += 'Name : ' + this.getName() + '<br/>';
    html += 'Date of Birth : ' +
this.getDob().toString() + '<br/>';
    html += 'Address : ' + this.getAddress() + '<br/>';
    html += 'City : ' + this.getCity();
    html += '</p>'
    return html;
  }
}
```

The above is a rewrite of the user object declaration, now we have a set of getter and setter methods. It might look like a lot of code but on close scrutiny it's just a lot of getter and setter methods, i.e. one method for each property. Note that the getDob method actually creates a date object and assigns it to the dob property. Plus we also changed the getHTML function of the user object so it returns a more comprehensive description of the user.

Let's fix the form so it now takes in all the fields.

```
frm.onsubmit = function(){
    var usr = new
user(document.getElementById('name').value);

    usr.setDob(day.options[day.selectedIndex].value,
month.options[month.selectedIndex].value,
```

```
year.options[year.selectedIndex].value);


usr.setAddress(document.getElementById('address').value
);
  usr.setCity(document.getElementById('city').value);

  theList.add(usr);

  ul.innerHTML = theList.getHTML();
  return false;
}
```

Run the above code, add in the details and you can now
see that all of the details are being displayed. This in its
own is a very comprehensive application. However lets
take it a little bit further.

Removing users.

We have a fully functional form here that adds and
displays added users at will. However we need to add the
ability to remove an existing user. Think about adding a
link to each element added that says remove. Clicking this
link would remove the element from the list. This means
that we need to create an a element and attach an onclick
event handler to it that would remove the element from the
array. For this let's redo the users getHTML function a bit.
Currently it returns a chunk of html, let's fix it so it returns
a node.

```
this.getHTML = function(){
  node = document.createElement('p');
```

```
    node.setAttribute('style', 'padding:5px; border:1px
solid #ccc;');
    span = document.createElement('span');
    span.innerHTML = 'Name : ' + this.getName() +
'<br/>';
    span.innerHTML += 'Date of Birth : ' +
this.getDob().toString() + '<br/>';
    span.innerHTML += 'Address : ' + this.getAddress()
+ '<br/>';
    span.innerHTML += 'City : ' + this.getCity();

    node.appendChild(span);
    return node;
  }
```

As you can see we created a few elements using
the `document.createElement` function. Then we
treated each individual element as a node. By doing this
we can assign event handlers and code which you couldn't
do with just passing in raw HTML. Now we also have to
adjust our list object. Currently the html property takes a
string of HTML. Let's fix it so we don't have to store a
bunch of html or nodes consistently and instead rewrite the
lists objects getHTML function so it returns the node for a
single element which is passed to it. We'll also rewrite the
add function of the list to pass to it both the element to add
as well as the dom unordered list element to append to.

We will also need to adjust the code in the form handler so
that the list is populated with nodes instead of plain html:

```
function list(){

  this.list = [];
  this.html = '' // we won't be using this now
```

```javascript
  this.add = function(elem, ul){
    this.list.push(elem);
    ul.appendChild(this.getHTML(elem))
    // this.buildHTML(elem); // delete this line
  }

  this.buildHTML = function(elem){ // get rid of this
for now
  }

  this.getHTML = function(elem){
    usr = elem.getHTML(); // get the users generated
node
    li = document.createElement('li');
    li.appendChild(usr);
    rm = document.createElement('a');
    rm.innerHTML = '(remove)';
    rm.setAttribute('href', '#');
    rm.onclick = function(){
      alert('delete me');
    }

    li.appendChild(rm);

    return li;
  }


  this.remove = function(index){
    this.list.splice(index, 1);
  }

  this.get = function(index){
    this.list[index];
  }
}

// in the form handler
frm.onsubmit = function(){
  var usr = new
user(document.getElementById('name').value);
```

```
    usr.setDob(day.options[day.selectedIndex].value,
month.options[month.selectedIndex].value,
year.options[year.selectedIndex].value);


usr.setAddress(document.getElementById('address').value
);
    usr.setCity(document.getElementById('city').value);

    theList.add(usr, ul);

    return false;
}
```

This may seem like a lot of code, but in fact if you break it
all down you can clearly see that we've made every
element into a node. You could not do that with raw html.
Run the code and you should see as you add entries the list
is populated. Click on the remove link against an element.
It seems like we have yet to code for the remove link. Let's
go back to our list object and work on the remove link
handler in the getHTML method.

```
    this.getHTML = function(elem){
        usr = elem.getHTML(); // get the users generated
node
        li = document.createElement('li');
        li.appendChild(usr);

        rm = document.createElement('a');
        rm.innerHTML = '(remove)';
        rm.setAttribute('href', '#');
        rm.onclick = function(){

this.parentNode.parentNode.removeChild(this.parentNode)
;
        }
```

```
    li.appendChild(rm);

    return li;
}
```

Run the code above, and click on the remove links now.
The element is removed from the unordered list in this
example. If you notice in the remove links handler we've
used the removeChild method of the parent node of the list
element. In this case the parent of the remove link was the
list element, and the parent of the li element was
the ul element. Parent elements can remove child
elements.

This is all very well but we have a problem here. We've
only deleted the element from the html's unordered list, it
still exists in the list objects list property. To remove it
from there, we need to know the index of the
corresponding element in the list. We can do this by
passing in the index of the element in the getHTML
method. Remember we are calling the getHTML method
when adding a node so it's easy to get the latest index to
pass to the function.

```
    this.getHTML = function(elem, index){
       usr = elem.getHTML(); // get the users generated
node
       li = document.createElement('li');
       li.appendChild(usr);

       rm = document.createElement('a');
       rm.innerHTML = '(remove)';
       rm.setAttribute('href', '#');
       rm.onclick = function(){

this.parentNode.parentNode.removeChild(this.parentNode)
```

```
;
        this.remove(index);
    }

    li.appendChild(rm);

    return li;
}
```

Your entire JavaScript code should look like this:

```javascript
function user(name) {
  this.name = name;
  this.dob = '';
  this.address = '';
  this.city = '';

  this.getName = function(){
    return this.name;
  }

  this.getCity = function(){
    return this.city;
  }

  this.getAddress = function(){
    return this.address;
  }

  this.getDob = function(){
    return this.dob;
  }

  this.setName = function(name){
    this.name = name;
  }

  this.setCity = function(city){
    this.city = city;
  }
```

```javascript
  this.setAddress = function(address){
    this.address = address;
  }

  this.setDob = function(day, month, year){
    this.dob = new Date(day, month, year);
  }

  this.getHTML = function(){
    node = document.createElement('p');
    node.setAttribute('style', 'padding:5px; border:1px
solid #ccc;');
    span = document.createElement('span');
    span.innerHTML = 'Name : ' + this.getName() +
'<br/>';
    span.innerHTML += 'Date of Birth : ' +
this.getDob().toString() + '<br/>';
    span.innerHTML += 'Address : ' + this.getAddress()
+ '<br/>';
    span.innerHTML += 'City : ' + this.getCity();

    node.appendChild(span);
    return node;
  }
}


function list(){

  this.list = [];

  this.add = function(elem, ul){
    this.list.push(elem);
    ul.appendChild(this.getHTML(elem),
(this.list.length - 1)); // note we pass the latest
index which is the last index of the array where the
element is
  }
```

```javascript
  this.getHTML = function(elem, index){
    usr = elem.getHTML(); // get the users generated
node
    li = document.createElement('li');
    li.appendChild(usr);

    rm = document.createElement('a');
    rm.innerHTML = '(remove)';
    rm.setAttribute('href', '#');
    rm.onclick = function(){

this.parentNode.parentNode.removeChild(this.parentNode)
;
      this.remove(index);
    }

    li.appendChild(rm);

    return li;
  }


  this.remove = function(index){
    this.list.splice(index, 1);
  }

  this.get = function(index){
    this.list[index];
  }
}


day = document.getElementById('dob_day');

for(i=1;i<31;i++){
  op = document.createElement('option');
  op.setAttribute('value', i);
  op.innerHTML = i;
  day.appendChild(op);
}
```

```javascript
month = document.getElementById('dob_month');

for(i=0; i<=11; i++){
  op = document.createElement('option');
  op.setAttribute('value', i);
  op.innerHTML = i+1;
  month.appendChild(op);
}

var d = new Date();
var current_year = d.getFullYear();

year = document.getElementById('dob_year');

for(i=current_year; i>=(current_year - 100); i--){
  op = document.createElement('option');
  op.setAttribute('value', i);
  op.innerHTML = i;
  year.appendChild(op);
}


var frm = document.getElementById('theForm');
var theList = new list();

frm.onsubmit = function(){
  var usr = new
user(document.getElementById('name').value);

  ul =  document.getElementById('ourList');
  usr.setDob(day.options[day.selectedIndex].value,
month.options[month.selectedIndex].value,
year.options[year.selectedIndex].value);


usr.setAddress(document.getElementById('address').value
);
  usr.setCity(document.getElementById('city').value);

  theList.add(usr, ul);
```

```
    return false;
}
```

Validate Validate and Validate again

This is a pretty useful application you've just built. But its very error prone, we need to make sure that the information entered is valid to begin with. To start with we need to make sure that the name, city and address fields are not empty. We could put all this validation logic in the form's handler, but that goes against the idea of object oriented programming. Shouldn't the user object be the one to tell us whether the information provided to it was valid or not? Makes a lot of sense now that you think of it, let's then add a simple function to the user object declaration that checks if all the above three fields are not empty. It returns a boolean value indicating whether the user object created is valid or not. If the object is valid then we'll append it to the list, if not, we'll alert with an error message.

Add the following in your user object:

```
this.isValid = function(){
  errors = [];
  if(this.name.trim() == ''){
    errors.push('Name is required');
  }
  if(this.city.trim() == ''){
    errors.push('City is required');
  }
  if(this.address.trim() == ''){
    errors.push('Address is required');
```

```
        }

        if(errors.length > 0){
          alert(errors.join(','));
          return false;
        }else{
          return true;
        }

    }
```

This is a simple function that checks if the listed properties are not empty. An invalid element would result in a boolean false and a nasty alert message. Make the following adjustment to your form handler:

```
frm.onsubmit = function(){
  var usr = new
user(document.getElementById('name').value);

  ul =  document.getElementById('ourList');
  usr.setDob(day.options[day.selectedIndex].value,
month.options[month.selectedIndex].value,
year.options[year.selectedIndex].value);


usr.setAddress(document.getElementById('address').value
);
  usr.setCity(document.getElementById('city').value);

  if(usr.isValid()){  // if usr.isValid returns true
then add it to the list
    theList.add(usr, ul);
  }
  return false;
}
```

Run the code again, try to add some incomplete entries. You should be greeted with an error message. Now you've implemented some sort of validation in your form. And all of this is handled straight in the browser using nothing but good old JavaScript and plain HTML.

Conclusion

This exercise in itself is a powerful example of what you can do with JavaScript. There is a whole lot more than can be covered, a lot of possibilities with JavaScript that we've hardly even scratched the surface of. But hopefully after going through this book, at this stage you're at a level where you now can confidently code using native JavaScript. The concepts you have learnt in this book cover the basic foundation upon which advanced concepts are based.

As you start programming you'll come across numerous libraries that really speed up the work and can accomplish a lot more in a single line of code than could have been done with the native JavaScript that we've studied. Point being is that once you know how to use the basics, you'll definitely have a greater appreciation for how new JavaScript libraries make even basic JavaScripting a whole lot easier.

The exercises in this book aren't a one off, there is lots of practice involved in becoming a good programmer. You've outgrown your training wheels and now you're more than ready to take on actual projects and learn as you work.

Here is to your success and to years of great coding.

31115617R00131

Made in the USA
Lexington, KY
15 February 2019